Comhairle Contae
Átha Cliath Theas
South Dublin County Council

WAY
MANRESA
DISCOVERIES ALONG THE
IGNATIAN CAMINO

BRENDAN McMANUS SJ

First published 2020 by Loyola Press, Chicago
www.loyolapress.com

This edition published 2020 by Messenger Publications
Messenger Publications,
37 Leeson Place, Dublin D02 E5V0
www.messenger.ie

ISBN 9781788123266

This book has been approved by the Irish Jesuit censor, process completed through the Irish Jesuit Curia office, Milltown Park, Dublin, 2017.

Scripture quotations are from New Revised Standard Version Bible: Catholic Edition, copyright © 1989, 1993 National Council of the Churches of Christ in the United States of America. Used by permission. All rights reserved worldwide.

Disclaimer: I have tried to recreate events, locales, and conversations from my memories of them. In order to maintain their anonymity, in some instances, I have changed the names of individuals and places, and I may have changed some identifying characteristics and details such as physical properties, occupations, and places of residence.

Designed by Messenger Publications Design Department
Typeset in Adobe Garamond Pro, Akzidenz Groteske & Charlemange
Printed by Hussar Books

Original title: The Way to Manresa
Photo insert art credits: All photos by Brendan McManus, SJ, except the MAGIS 2016 concert photo by Jakub Nicieja. Used by permission.
p. viii The Ignatian Camino Route map courtesy of José Luis Irriberri, SJ.

AMDG

CONTENTS

The Ignatian Camino Route... viii

Pilgrim Prologue: The Desire to Be Open ix

1 Blinded by the Light 1

2 Walking on Sunshine 5

3 Seeking Sanctuary.. 17

4 Misty Mountain Hop 27

5 Cold Mountain Mud 37

6 The Hard Road... 47

7 The Doctor's Advice... 57

8 Rioja, Utopia.. 65

9 Against the Flow 73

10 The Lonely Vigil... 83

11 The Cave of the Conversion... 93

12 The Divine Architect 103

13 Back to Black.. 111

14 The Good Doctor.. 117

15 Escaping the Crutches 127

16 Beating the Belfast Blues 141

17 The Pope and I.. 151

18 Winter's End... 163

Epilogue: Feeling Good 175

Ignatian Tips for "Feeling Good" 185

Appendix: Praying with Failure... 187

Playlist of Songs to Accompany This Book 189

Select References and Recommended Reading 191

Acknowledgments.. 194

About the Author... 196

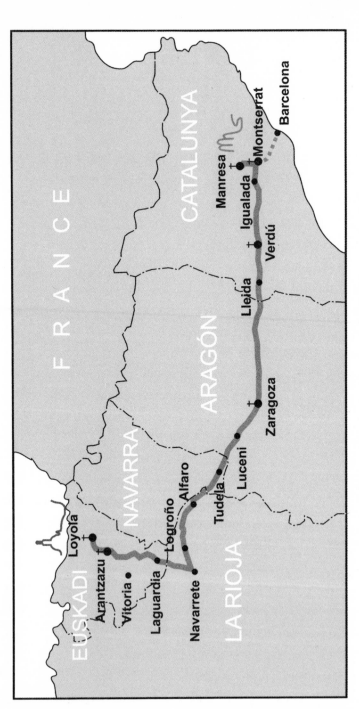

THE IGNATIAN CAMINO ROUTE

PILGRIM PROLOGUE:
THE DESIRE TO BE OPEN

Like many organizations and movements, the Society of Jesus, whose members are known as the Jesuits, is based on the experience of its founder, St. Ignatius of Loyola. People have varying stereotypical perceptions of Ignatius as the counterreformer, the grim ascetic, the great mystic, or the military ruler of a Catholic order. However, it is in reading the account of his life that he dictated and the Constitutions of the Jesuits, and in piecing together Ignatius's correspondence that we come to understand Ignatius principally as a pilgrim. In 1522, he cast off the trappings of his old life and limped around Europe as a poor beggar trying to discover what God wanted for him. Determined to learn about the "things of God," he threw himself heart and soul into the pilgrim experience. To his own surprise, he found himself having to learn to moderate his excessive tendencies, given his impulsive nature. Ignatius underwent a painful relearning, especially in Manresa, like a child at school again, to come to the realization that he did not need to engage in excessive penance or harsh asceticism to please God. Ignatius's great insight was to learn how to be open, to drop his own agenda and follow the path that God revealed to him.

His famous spiritual masterpiece, the *Spiritual Exercises*—a set of spiritual exercises collected into a book—is based on his own itinerant experiences, and it offers others similar practical pathways to be able to find freedom in life and God in all things.[1] For that reason, Ignatius insists that after Jesuits in training (novices) complete the Spiritual Exercises, they undertake a walking pilgrimage of some weeks, asking along the way for food and accommodation. This experience integrates life and faith and engenders a new trust in providence, which shapes one's priorities and life decisions. Living as a pilgrim and achieving an inner freedom inspired by St. Ignatius is something to which every Jesuit or Ignatian follower aspires. The hardest thing is letting go of our own plans and will, being flexible and subverting our ego to God's desire for us. This gift, called spiritual freedom, which must be experienced rather than rationalized about, is most easily found on the road.

Going on pilgrimage is an ancient tradition. In medieval Europe, pilgrims would leave the safety of their own homes to travel to Rome, Jerusalem, or Santiago de Compostela in repentance, for an intention, or to fulfill a promise. This meant putting themselves at the mercy of the elements, possibly risking life and limb, and depending on the hospitality of others. The renewed popularity since the 1980s of making a pilgrimage along northern Spain's Camino de Santiago—or the Way of St. James—as well as society's contemporary fascination with pilgrimage in all its forms is perhaps an attempt to recover ancient values, basic humanity, and a hint of the divine. Either way, it is a step into the mystery of the unknown and opening oneself to providence.

For myself, pilgrimage has been a constant theme in my Jesuit life and a place where I go to get clarity and find answers to questions.

---

1. Reading the *Spiritual Exercises* of St. Ignatius directly is a frustrating affair, as they were originally written as guidelines for retreat directors who have to adapt them to persons and contexts as needed; hence, they seem turgid and obscure for many readers. Instead, I suggest some of the excellent guides to and interpretations of the *Spiritual Exercises*, such as the Fleming, O'Leary, and Silf books mentioned in the recommended reading section.

There are three significant pilgrimage walks mentioned in this text, which are intimately connected to each other.

1. In 1993, when I was training as a Jesuit novice, I was a poor pilgrim walking across northeastern Spain in the footsteps of Ignatius, visiting the key sites connected with his conversion process. This journey from Ignatius's birthplace, Loyola, to Manresa, where he wrote the *Spiritual Exercises*, would subsequently become the Ignatian Camino but was then unstructured and ad hoc. The issue for me at that time was confirmation of my decision to join the Jesuits, which arrived in the form of an eleventh-hour "mountaintop" experience. This profound encounter shaped my prayer and spirituality and subsequently motivated me to organize groups walking Irish pilgrimage trails as a way of replicating the pilgrim's process of becoming free.

2. In 2011, I walked the widely known Camino de Santiago as a way of dealing with grief, and this led to the publication of my book *Redemption Road*. In that book I worked to combine the spirit of Ignatius (finding God in everyday experience) with the ancient route of the Camino (pilgrimage as a journey of discovery), focusing on themes of purifying the soul, shedding baggage of all sorts, and becoming free. This book unexpectedly also launched me into the ministry of suicide bereavement.

3. In 2015, I returned to Spain to walk again in Ignatius's footsteps, retracing the same sixteenth-century journey from his birthplace, Loyola, to Manresa. This time, however, the trail was newly organized, launched by the Spanish Jesuits in 2010 as the *Camino Ignaciano*, or the Ignatian Camino.[2] It will mark the 500th anniversary of Ignatius's journey in 2022. Though

---

2. www.caminoignaciano.org/en

not strictly a "Santiago" Camino, it uses the same system of way
markers, a website, and a guidebook, thus marrying the Camino
tradition with the actual towns and landscapes where Ignatius
himself passed through and spent time. It goes east across Spain
and actually runs in the opposite direction to the famous French
Camino de Santiago, and at one stage between Logroño and
Navarrete, pilgrims share the same trail.

This book details my adventures on the Ignatian Camino in 2015
where, finding myself caught up in a whirl of bereavement work, I
recognized the need to reconnect with the sources of my vocation
through the Ignatian sites, as well as recover the sense of peace and
inner balance from my 2011 Camino to Santiago. The Ignatian
Camino seemed the perfect marriage of the two, a Camino-style trail
with a distinctly Ignatian flavor. This time I had fifteen days that
would take me about halfway, and I would take a train to finish in
Manresa. Precisely because of my previous pilgrimage experiences, my
expectations were very high. I remembered the great joys and hard-
won insights but conveniently forgot the arduous process of arriving
there. Beyond a shadow of a doubt, I knew that I would find answers
on the trail, however, and I knew I would have to abandon myself to
the vagaries of God's plan. Spiritual freedom would be key in abandoning my own priorities or resistance in order to accept God's superior and challenging plan. On the trail, though, life is unpredictable,
and anything can happen . . .

1

BLINDED BY THE LIGHT

In anticipation I woke earlier than I had planned. Quickly stuffing everything into my backpack, thinking about nothing but being back "on the Camino," I could hardly contain myself. After a trying first day's journey from Loyola to Zumárraga, I was eager to continue on to Aranzazu. I stepped out into the cool predawn on the outskirts of town and breathed deeply as I began my second day's walking. The luxury of sixteen days away on the Camino Ignaciano—the Ignatian Way! Opening up my phone's GPS app, I noticed a shortcut. By taking the new bypass, I would avoid going back across the valley into the industrial town of Zumárraga and get directly onto the route. In fact, it was so close I could see the street lamps marking the path a half mile away. "A smart and devious shortcut," I thought, feeling pleased with myself as I strode down the hard shoulder.

It was a little unpleasant at first, shoved into the shoulder by the odd car that roared past, but the footpath was getting closer, and I would meet it in a matter of minutes. I checked the route on my phone again and shivered in the cold. The forecast was good, and I knew in a few hours I would be sweltering. I picked up my speed to cover the last 300 yards. A car came toward me, full headlights on. Momentarily blinded, I stepped into a pothole at the road's edge. The next thing I knew, my ankle rolled and I found myself falling. It seemed that I was floating for several seconds, and then my knee hit the unforgiving asphalt. There was nothing but silence as I went over forward, my backpack following over my head. I shrieked in agony as the shredding of nerves forced the pain message to my brain. White noise and tinnitus suddenly roared, drowning out all thought. The only thing I remember was internally screaming at the driver, "For pity's sake, stop!" as he blasted past, oblivious. To him, I must have looked like a tumble of color and limbs at the side of the road, a momentary distraction, unimportant.

It was some time before I came around from the shock and was able to pick myself up off the ground. There was a torrent of throbbing pain in my right knee. When I put my hand down, I felt my knee was warm and greasy, then realized it was blood. I limped over to a streetlight and sat on a low wall to survey the damage. *Relax*, I thought, *it's probably just scraped and bloodied; let's see what's underneath this mess.* I washed the cuts on my knee with my water bottle and noticed that the knuckles on my left hand were skinned too, from holding onto my phone. Everything hurt, especially my pride, but on the positive side, nothing seemed broken, all my gear was intact, and I was still able to move.

I took a moment to curse myself for my stupidity. Taking an unnecessary shortcut, half-asleep, and falling in the dark, and this on the second morning! If I was lucky, depending on what the damage was, I would get away with this minor fall, a temporary inconvenience. Even though my knee hurt more, it was the skinned knuckles that were a constant visual reminder of my shortsightedness: saving a few minutes and protecting a stupid phone had cost me dearly.

In the brightening morning light, I looked back down the arterial road that was my shortcut, wanting to start the day over. In my rush to get on the trail, I hadn't paid attention to what was going on around me. It was a rookie Camino error, and now I would have to face up to the consequences. Still, I knew I had to get myself to a medical clinic to get checked out. As it was so early, barely seven o'clock, there was no one around. I decided to walk the short distance, a mile and a half, to the next town.

Injury clouds judgment, and a shock can cause immobility, I knew. Steeling myself, I started moving again, gasping with the waves of pain. The first few steps were excruciating as I put weight back on my knee and struggled to stay upright. My limbs felt wooden and hard, stiff with shock and inflammation. After some minutes, things did get better, the sharp pain dissolved, and I could walk, albeit with a limp. *Small steps, one foot in front of the other*, I thought.

Back on the Camino path, I hobbled along as best I could, trying to convince myself that my leg was getting better and that a doctor would sort everything out. Desolation, frustration, anger with myself, and self-pity all threatened to overwhelm me, but I managed to shrug them off. This could be a serious situation, so I focused my thoughts on reaching a clinic and banished everything else. The temptation was to be immobilized by feelings of self-pity, for example, but this was not a time for wavering or delaying but for acting decisively. This bleak walk in the half-light was exacerbated by the ugliest of industrial areas surrounding the Camino path. Walls, warehouses, and the harsh fluorescent flare of security lights depressed my spirit. My heart at first jumped for joy at the sight of two men approaching, but then their two dogs following on filled me with fear. I suddenly felt very vulnerable and alone. Without a stick, cut and bruised, I felt exposed. But I was committed, and there was no other way but through them.[3] One dog came bounding down excitedly and, jumping up, tried to lick my hands. With horror, I realized he could taste blood. The other

---

3. This was effectively a "survival" situation, where, because of the desolation I was feeling after the fall, I was tempted to give up, but sticking to my decision to get help was the thing to do (don't make a change in desolation; SE 319).

dog became interested too; I was rooted to the spot, unable to escape. Normally a dog lover, in that moment I saw only dangerous wolves. Eventually the owners called them off, unaware of the drama I felt, and I summoned the strength to ask directions for a café.

Soon, I came across a café for truckers that was open and decided to stop. I was in bad need of some food to combat my growing hunger. I limped down from the path through a car park to where a group of men were gathered outside the café, smoking and drinking coffee. The bartender, a man with kind eyes, took my order and pointed upstairs to the *servicios*, or restrooms. Ascending the stairs cost me dearly. I hung onto the handrail for support, gasping at the demands of my knee. When I took time to wash everything thoroughly, I could see clearly the cuts on my knees and my skinned knuckles. *Superficial*, I kept telling myself. Back downstairs I devoured a *café con leche* and some small bar snacks, *pinchos*, oblivious to everything else.

2

WALKING ON SUNSHINE

Two weeks earlier, a sunny afternoon had drawn me into St. Anne's Cathedral, in Belfast, Northern Ireland. I was praying for my imminent Camino trip and reflecting on my motives for doing it. I struggled to get my head straight, experiencing very different motivations.[4] As I gazed upward, the stained-glass window high up in the nave drew my eye. Radiating every bright color, it seemed to me like an image of the Resurrection, the sun and light streaming in from above. *That's what I want*, I thought, *to revisit that amazing memory of the Camino.* My eyes skipped over the less attractive crown of thorns below with its muted hues; this walk would be free of accidents or any suffering, I assured myself. The guide later told me this window represented the Trinity, which greatly consoled me, as the Trinity was a key element of Ignatius's prayer. The window revealed the close relationship of Father, Son, and Holy Spirit, all looking outward, not inward. Somehow, I was being invited in; God was reaching out to me and inviting me to go on a journey. This loving God, a community of persons, would accompany me on my pilgrimage and teach me new things.

---

4. Making good decisions is complicated by the fact that we are made up of conflicting thoughts, emotions, and desires that can easily derail us. The challenge is to accept the messiness of this, ask for help, and try to find a way through. Michael Ivens, SJ, *Understanding the Spiritual Exercises* (Leominster, UK: Gracewing, 1998), 208–9.

I offered my upcoming pilgrimage on the Camino to the Trinity, praying in gratitude for what I had experienced during my previous pilgrimage and asking to taste more of that same joy, freedom, and providence. I would be walking the same Ignatian Way route that I had done as a novice some twenty-one years before, and I especially wanted to do the all-night vigil to Our Lady of Montserrat that Ignatius himself had done.[5] I was filled with the joy and anticipation of walking in the footsteps of Ignatius and reliving his momentous 400-mile route from Loyola to Manresa in northeastern Spain. This time, I could do only about half of the route, so finishing would have been impossible. I planned to walk as far as I could, at least halfway, and get a train for the rest. I knew too well the dangers of pushing too hard, and I promised myself I would be more discerning this time.

The day of my departure saw a punishing start at two o'clock in the morning to get the bus to Dublin Airport. On the way we got lost outside of Belfast, and the driver had to ask directions from the passengers, even stopping a pedestrian! Eventually, we took off at great speed, and I began to feel queasy on the top deck. I thought back to the farewell meal the night before with a Jesuit colleague in my community who had given me a lot of advice on the route. Having walked it multiple times, he filled me in on various route alternatives, recommended certain accommodation options, and clarified daily walking distances.

When I disembarked in Bilbao, I was heartened by the number of hikers heading for the main Camino de Santiago routes, the French and the northern routes being very close. The unmistakable signs were purposeful striding, scallop shells, and minimal-weight hiking

---

5. José Luis Iriberri and Chris Lowney, *Guía del Camino Ignaciano*, 3rd ed. (Bilbao: Mensajero, 2016), www.caminoignaciano.org/en; Brendan McManus, SJ, "Ignatian Pilgrimage: The Inner Journey—Loyola to Manresa on Foot," *The Way* 49, no. 3 (July 2010): 95–108.

gear. I introduced myself to two young Irish women I'd seen on the plane; they were doing the northern route to Santiago that I had done four years prior. Their Camino enthusiasm was infectious. I filled them in as best I could on what lay ahead and wished them well. My Camino, the Ignatian Camino, was a little-known new arrival among the Spanish pilgrimage routes. Following in the footsteps of St. Ignatius, it connected the places intimately related to his story, such as Loyola and Manresa. This route, instead of heading westward towards Santiago like the other Camino routes, goes eastward to Manresa, the great Ignatian destination.[6] I had walked across the country following Ignatius's route in 1994 as a Jesuit novice, but now the path was newly dedicated and replete with way markers, its own "pilgrim passport," and various hostels along the way. I could hardly wait for this Camino experience and the many Ignatian sites in one perfect pilgrimage!

From Bilbao, the normal two-hour bus journey to Loyola took a detour along the coast through San Sebastián, but I figured out a more direct route via Eibar, deep into the steep mountains of the Basque Country. On the bus, I fell into conversation with a very friendly local hiker who tipped me off that there was no connecting bus from Eibar to Loyola on Sundays. He found me an alternative route on his smartphone, which unfortunately meant taking a train back to the coast and then another bus to Loyola. My own detour had cost me half a day, but I enjoyed the providential adventures nonetheless. It was a familiar learning moment on the Camino, letting go of

---

6. Though this route had been walked by various Jesuits, especially novices as part of their pilgrimage training, it was formally launched by the Spanish Jesuits in 2010 as an official route, using Camino-style way markers and a guidebook. The route is currently being developed, however, and certain aspects are still under construction. Ignatian pilgrims meet Camino de Santiago hikers going in the opposite direction. Walking with Inigo—The Ignatian Camino; Following in the footsteps of Saint Ignatius of Loyola. www.caminoignaciano.org/en/.

control and personal plans. The payoff was that I got to pass through majestic mountains, an exercise in awareness and being present to beauty.[7]

I reached Loyola in the late afternoon and asked the bus driver to drop me off early so I could savor the riverside walk to the Sanctuary. A complex of buildings, including the basilica, contains the original Loyola castle, the birthplace of Ignatius. The dome is visible from some miles away. For Jesuits, Loyola is home. It is the home of our founder, St. Ignatius of Loyola, but also the physical locus of his transformation. Ignatius had his conversion experience here in 1521. Made an invalid by a traumatic injury that affected both legs, his dreams of being a chivalrous knight were in tatters. Grimly holding onto the vanity and desires of his old life, he had no idea of the great plans God had in store for him.

While immobilized in bed, Ignatius stumbled upon the simple yet profound insight that God was communicating directly with him through his moods.[8] God was using Ignatius's habitual daydreaming not to fuel his escapism and fantasy, as he was given to chivalry and romance, but to effect a change of heart. Rather than giving his heart to an earthly nobility, he was in thrall to a divine leader. The original Loyola castle, encased as it is within a larger building, loomed large in my imagination. The actual room of the conversion, his place of suffering and insight, was firmly before me in my mind.

---

7. Ignatian awareness is about listening to and perceiving the world, understanding that life has meaning and that God is communicating with us always. Prayer becomes all-inclusive, a conscious and personal relationship with God. W. A. Barry, "Prayer as Conscious Relationship," in *An Ignatian Spirituality Reader: Contemporary Writings on St. Ignatius of Loyola, the Spiritual Exercises, Discernment, and More*, ed. George W. Traub (Chicago: Loyola Press, 2008), 99–103.

8. There is a deeper level to feelings that, when looked at with silence and space, reveal something of how God is calling us. Franz Meures, SJ, "The Affective Dimension of Discerning and Deciding," *Review of Ignatian Spirituality* 39, no. 1 (2008): 60–77.

Twenty-one years ago, I had started my pilgrimage from that very room with a solemn midnight vigil for safe passage as a novice walking across Spain.

Now, as I crossed the Urola River, the basilica's impressive Baroque façade and imposing avenue swung into view. The place of my heart's desire was before me; I was on the journey at last. When I accessed the main reception by the old castle, the local woman couldn't have been more helpful. She gave me lots of information on the Ignatian Camino, including the essential "pilgrim passport" that had to be stamped each day to verify my progress. After settling into my room, I went down for dinner. The dark, wood-paneled dining room was buzzing with an international group of Jesuits who, like me, were irresistibly drawn to Loyola. It was a great joy to meet some Jesuits from India and Sri Lanka and reunite with others from Latin America whom I had met previously. That evening, a man from Colombia arranged for a tour of Blessed Brother Francisco Gárate's house, right next to Loyola. The Jesuit brother is remembered for doing ordinary things well: showing hospitality, being a doorkeeper, and caring for students. Simple living, humility, and great devotion marked his dwelling. I soon excused myself for the real treat: night prayer alone in the Chapel of the Conversion.[9] The wood floors smelled of wax and preservative, triggering powerful memories and emotions for me. Back in 1994, I had been seeking confirmation of the massive move into religious life; the most heartfelt prayer of my life had been in that room, asking for help with the forthcoming

---

9. Called the Examen, night prayer means looking back over the day as if watching a movie of it with a wise and compassionate friend. The simple act of reflecting on experience reveals the significance of different events, moments of light and also shadow. This process allows one to see how conscious one has been of God's presence, savoring the good moments, learning from the bad ones, and trying to live a better day tomorrow (SE 43). Timothy M. Gallagher, *The Examen Prayer: Ignatian Wisdom for Our Lives Today* (New York: Crossroad, 2006).

pilgrimage and my decision to join the Jesuits. I always seem to return to this: petitioning grace and guidance out of great emotional vulnerability. Now I was facing another journey into the unknown, wondering what other transitions or plans God had in store for me. Alone in the dark in the room where Ignatius understood God's personal love for him—it was all I could do not to weep.

The next morning I awoke sore and miserable with a stomachache, something I ate hadn't agreed with me. I barely made it through early Mass. Feeling very sheepish in my hiking gear with a readied backpack, I went back to bed after breakfast. I retired as gracefully as I could, frustrated but patiently working through my regret over postponing my start and reflecting that God must have something better in store for me. I tried to focus on prioritizing my health and well-being over my will.[10] Later, once I had rested, I was drawn into the deliciously cool garden by the bright sunshine that was infusing everything with new life. The craggy peaks all around me appeared to envelop the sanctuary in their arms like a mother.

St. Ignatius of Loyola was born in 1491, to a family of minor nobility in the Basque Country in northern Spain. As a young man, Ignatius was impulsive, vain, and proud, getting into brawls on a number of occasions. In 1521, in a battle with the French at Pamplona, Ignatius demonstrated enormous courage against impossible odds. His legs were seriously damaged by a cannonball during the battle, and he had to be carried home to Loyola on a stretcher. After coming close to death following a brutal operation to reset his broken right leg, he devotedly prayed to St. Peter

---

10. Ignatius emphasizes letting go of things that are not good for us, even minor compulsions or addictions, anything that prevents us from living life fully. He calls this spiritual freedom (SE 21).

and had a miraculous recovery. During the many months of his injury-induced immobility and recuperation, Ignatius noticed some key differences in his moods. Out of boredom he was reading the lives of Christ and the saints, in contrast to his normal chivalrous and heroic daydreaming. While the latter left him feeling dry and empty afterward, imagining himself outdoing the saints in asceticism left him happy and content. While mulling over these inner movements, Ignatius had the insight that they were God's direct communication with him.

From the time of his recovery from his injured leg until his death, Ignatius walked with a limp. Against his brother's wishes, Ignatius left home as soon as he was well enough; he had a fierce desire to leave the trappings of his old life behind and become an itinerant pilgrim. Still unskilled in reading his inner moods or movements, and given to impulsive extremes, it took a long time for him to learn the art of reflection and balance. Traveling across Europe by foot and begging became Ignatius's preferred way of life, and much of what would later become the *Spiritual Exercises* was based on the experiences he honed during this period as a "pilgrim," as he described himself. His first journey from Loyola to Manresa—what is today the route of the Ignatian Camino—was where he learned the slow process of integrating faith and life. Those first two years were arguably the most formative time, especially in Manresa, which saw the maturing of his spiritual life, when he was "taught like a child by a schoolteacher."[11] This art of listening to the inner movements of the Spirit, refined by his experiences on the road, led him eventually

---

11. Ignatius's conversion did not happen in one blinding moment but in a process over years. Brendan Comerford, SJ, *The Pilgrim's Story: The Life and Spirituality of St. Ignatius Loyola* (Dublin: Messenger Publications, 2017), 25–26.

to formulate his insights into the *Spiritual Exercises* and teach others how to listen and decide. In 1540, Ignatius of Loyola, together with a close group of friends, founded the Jesuits, labeling them "contemplatives in action" because of the missionary focus they would have. Ignatius was elected the first head of the order, and he performed this administrative role from Rome until his death in 1556.

Praying in the Chapel of the Conversion that evening, I asked for energy and enthusiasm for setting out the next day. Seeing the burnished statue of Ignatius with his ecstatic face made something click for me: I needed some more reflective awareness in my life and to acknowledge how God works in my experience.[12] Not feeling well earlier that morning had given me important information and encouraged me to slow down and treat myself with more compassion. There was a lesson for me here, I knew, as I remembered how Ignatius swapped self-determination for sensitivity to the Holy Spirit. My brief setback had granted me a day of reflection, prepared me for the vagaries of existence on the Camino de Santiago, and forced me to slow down right from the start. The lessons of my previous time on the Camino were coming back to me, always hard won. Ignatius used to say that, even as an adult, he felt like a child being taught by God.[13] I had the slightly

---

12. Ignatius is sometimes described as the first psychologist, as he used human consciousness, the ability to observe ourselves and reflect on experience to draw meaning from it. Human subjectivity is the living within the human condition of emotions, perceptions, and sensations, which, though superficially confusing, do contain deeper affective and spiritual information. The Ignatian process of reflecting on experience means paying attention to the drawings or urgings of the Spirit at work in our profound longings or desires. Mark E. Thibodeaux, *God's Voice Within: The Ignatian Way to Discover God's Will* (Chicago: Loyola Press, 2010), 9.

13. Ignatius realized how close God was to him and how he himself was being reoriented and reeducated. Joseph N. Tylenda, SJ, *A Pilgrim's Journey: The Autobiography of Ignatius of Loyola* (Collegeville, MN: Liturgical Press, 1991), No. 27, pp. 35–36.

uncomfortable feeling that I was being taught as well, and I struggled to find the humility to be open to what I was supposed to be learning. I consoled myself by thinking that it took Ignatius many years to move from his own willfulness toward surrender to God's will.

Morning prayer in the darkened Chapel of the Conversion, at barely visible dawn, was a sacred moment. I prayed from my reality: "Into your hands, Lord, I commend myself and this walk."[14] When I was later alone on top of the main steps of the basilica, I celebrated my departure, Rocky Balboa-style, with an imaginary crowd. It was a cold early morning, but I knew a hot sun lurked just behind the shroud of mist. I adjusted my backpack straps, felt the reassuring weight on my back and shoulders, and settled into the rhythm of the road. I deliberately resisted the urge to race off at speed and took my time to search for the Camino signposts. A navigation app on my phone was a great help in getting started, but it irritatingly bleeped every time I went even slightly off course.

The asphalt path threaded a way through the trees, parallel to the Urola River. The mist was beginning to lift and also my spirits. My first pilgrimage landmark was in Azkoitia, some two miles out. I ignored the bleeping of my phone to visit a huge sixteenth-century Baroque church, Santa María La Real—all Baroque chunky pillars and domed ceilings. The sacristan took me under his wing and gave me a tour, including some welcome refreshments. He was called Jesús, and I thought to myself that Jesus himself would have been as hospitable. Jesús invited me to stay for Mass in Basque, and I was glad for the reminder to maintain a slow cadence and attend to spiritual things.

After Mass, back on the gravel trail, it was all uphill, an unusually consistent incline. Eventually I realized I was walking on an old

---

14. Using the words of Jesus on the cross in Luke 23:46, this is a powerful prayer of abandonment, of handing over, the ultimate "freedom" of placing oneself in God's hands (SE 297).

railway line that had been turned into a recreational trail for walkers and cyclists. It was a lovely walk, with iron bridges over rivers and a seemingly endless succession of tunnels blasted through the mountainside. Long and short, they were all well-lit, except for one dark exception when I had to use my phone as a flashlight.

I found a shady place between two tunnels to eat my picnic lunch in the vast Basque outdoors. A couple on bikes stopped and asked me to take their photo, and we chatted for a while. Seeing the scallop shell I carry from my previous pilgrimage to Santiago de Compostela, they told me I was far from the Camino de Santiago, but I explained that I was following the Ignatian Camino to Manresa. After we parted, I resolved that on this walk, I would acknowledge and greet everyone I met along the way.

After lunch, the temperature started to shoot up into the eighties, and with no more tunnels, I was exposed to the sun. I craved the shelter of the tunnels' shade and the early morning fog, which had spared me from baking in the heat. I considered a siesta, but my destination, Zumárraga, was very close. Eleven miles later and my feet were sore; the last mile seemed to go on forever. At one point, I stepped aside to let a cyclist pass, and to my annoyance, he didn't even acknowledge me. Clearly, I was getting tired, hungry, and cranky.

I trailed along into town, dripping sweat, and made directly for the town hall. The woman at the information desk, Raquel, couldn't have been nicer. She explained that there was no *albergue* in town, but there were three boardinghouses (*pensiones*) and a cheap hotel. She directed me to the nearby Tino's Bar. The bartender was a relative of one of the *pensión* owners. Tino himself was very helpful; he rang two *pensiones*, discovering there was no room in either. Mercifully, the third one turned out to have a room. I walked over to it and quickly paid for the room. Tired and showered, I collapsed into the mercifully cool bed for a rest.

Raquel had insisted earlier that I visit an old church nearby, Santa María Hermitage ("La Antigua"). I wasn't keen on more walking, but she had called it the "cathedral of hermitages" and said it was only twenty minutes away. The hillside walk was steep, cutting through an area of fortress-like houses and unrivaled views. Even at seven in the evening, the heat was punishing, and my clean T-shirt was soon sweaty. I caught up with two men also toiling up in the heat. One of them, Antonio, had been to Ireland and loved it—a big fan. The older of the two, Xavier, was more extroverted and engaging. I welcomed their company as a providential distraction from the heat on this walk.

The hermitage, which dated to the twelfth century, was a former fortified house of wood and stone. Its oak ceiling, trusses, and lofts created a womb-like warmth and stillness, much like how I imagined the original stable where the Holy Family stayed. As the tour guide explained the history of the building and especially the images and statues of Our Lady, I felt close to Ignatius. I was overjoyed to learn that he had prayed here in 1522 on his way to Arantzazu, which was my next planned stop. We spent over an hour at the hermitage, exploring the hallowed fortress-turned-church. As I prayed alone in a pew, I noticed the vivid background music that had been playing. It was the uilleann pipes, unmistakably Celtic, and it made the hair stand up on the back of my neck.[15] Music and moment combined to highlight an undefined spiritual significance. The music seemed the perfect "setting out" song, a soundtrack for leaving the past behind. I tried to imagine what Ignatius would have felt in this place, perhaps some sense of regret over the past and some tentative hope for the

---

15. This uilleann pipes track was Loreena McKennitt's cover of the Irish ballad "Bonny Portmore," from the 1991 album *The Visit*. The song is a lament over the loss of a great oak tree near Portmore Lough in County Antrim, felled by a storm in 1760, but later became emblematic of widespread deforestation.

future. Unbeknownst to him, though, at that time he was stepping over a threshold into a new life, directed by God.

Back at the *pensión*, I began to reminisce about the past few years and felt grateful for all I had received. I remembered my exceptional experience in 2011 on the Camino de Santiago and how that pilgrimage had helped me move forward from my grief over my brother's death by suicide. Since then, he has been with me in a new way as an encouraging voice and a constant companion, a source of great joy to me. Back in 2011, I had flown home from Santiago on a cloud of gratitude and well-being that had hardly dissipated since. My prayer remained intimate and spontaneous, such that I thought that this feeling of closeness would last forever. It was like I had a new life.[16]

This time on the Ignatian Camino would be a holiday, I determined, a temporary escape from my daily reality. Everything seemed to be shaping up as before, right down to the providential happenings of the previous two days. *Tomorrow, I'll be walking on sunshine*, I thought while switching off the light.

---

16. The icing on the cake was being able to write my book *Redemption Road*, which allowed me to travel the country and tell others about my experience on the road with God. These experiences also brought me to work in suicide bereavement, where I tried to help others going through a similar process. I had a great sense of providence, of God bringing good out of tragedy. This time on the Ignatian Camino, I was looking for a similar spiritual uplift and grace, conscious that there was something very wearing about the bereavement work, which, though valuable and rewarding, was personally demanding. Brendan McManus, SJ, *Redemption Road: From Grief to Peace through Walking the Camino de Santiago* (Chicago: Loyola Press, 2016).

3

SEEKING SANCTUARY

Without my having to say a word, the bartender discreetly asked how he could help. When I explained that I was looking for a doctor, he told me there was a medical clinic right in town. In my urgent need, it seemed that God was speaking through him.[17] I limped up the main square, my leg still stiff and painful. A woman from the Dominican Republic noticed my condition and went out of her way to show me to the clinic.

When I saw the doctor, he checked me out and examined my bloody knee. To my relief, he gave me the all-clear, saying the cuts were just superficial. He told me to take a day off and rest my swollen knee. *I got away with it,* I gleefully thought, *no significant injury! I'll be back walking in a day.* He sent me to the nurse to have my wounds dressed. The atmosphere was relaxed and jovial—when the nurses learned I could speak some Spanish, they began teasing me about what an unfortunate pilgrim I was, falling at the first hurdle. I joked that I needed bandages to elicit sympathy on the road. I was sorry to

---

17. This was to become a real feature of the walk, that people would continually give me good advice and directions that I needed to follow. Eventually I resolved to follow whatever reasonable advice people offered. Ignatius notes that God is working in and through all beings for good (SE 235–37).

leave the warmth and camaraderie of this little clinical oasis, but I had to get on my way.

Walking around the lovely little Basque town in the morning sunshine, I was grateful for many things, but mostly for having the chance to slow down. Finding a shady park bench, I stretched out my newly bandaged leg, thinking the pain had lessened considerably. *I'll be right as rain after a rest tomorrow*, I thought, thinking of resuming my walk the day after. I decided to travel via bus to the sanctuary of Arantzazu, my original destination for that day. By taking a bus to Oñate and another to the cliffside monastery, I could make up all the time I had lost from my injury, spend my day off there, and begin walking again the following day. *What a crazy day of ups and downs (mostly downs!)*, I thought.

I made my way down to the bus stop at the bottom of the square. As I was waiting for the bus, a car pulled up. To my amazement, it was the bartender again, asking how I was doing. Moved, I filled him in and thanked him profusely. But he made little of his kindness, waving it away with his hand. *This is something exceptional*, I thought, *treating a stranger with a hospitality worthy of the Gospels.*[18] With time on my hands, I looked around me and noticed all of a sudden many people using wheelchairs or walking with the aid of canes. Soberly, I reflected how much, and how quickly, my perception had changed in those few moments. I too often see the world as *I* am, not as *it* is; the day before I might not have even noticed all these people around me.

I gratefully collapsed into a bus seat, giving up all notions of completing the stage on foot. Taking the bus was so obviously the right decision at that point. Unlike my previous time on the Camino, where I agonized over taking public transportation, here I was done

---

18. The Gospel is about love in action, "faith working through love," and making a difference in the world. Pope Francis, *The Joy of the Gospel: Evangelii Gaudium* (Frederick, MD: Word among Us Press, 2014), nos. 34–39.

being a purist. In some Camino circles, taking any form of transportation is frowned upon, but I had learned the wisdom of being flexible and not so rule-driven.[19] I sat back and enjoyed the rugged heart of the Basque Country, a glory of hills, rock, and winding roads.

Eventually, we arrived in Oñate, which aptly means the "place of many hills." I found the tourism office, and a very helpful woman informed me there was no midweek bus to Arantzazu. My only option would be a taxi. While I figured things out, I decided to look around the town. Dating to the medieval period, Oñate has some impressive buildings, including the sixteenth-century University of the Holy Spirit (Sancti Spíritus), with its remarkable Renaissance-style façade. Nearby was the monastery of Bidaurreta and the Gothic Church of St. Michael. As I ate my lunch sitting in the main square, I was transported back in time to the world of Ignatius. The largely unchanged university's Renaissance-era architecture reflected Ignatius's cultural inheritance: an emphasis on education, humanism, and balance. The "architecture" of Ignatius's *Spiritual Exercises* reflects the same values of respect for the individual, flexible adaptation, return to sources (such as the Scriptures), and being open to the world. This made me feel concretely that God was present to me even then, working with me individually and nudging me toward decision and action. Taking my feeling as a sign to get going, I asked two men how to get to the Arantzazu sanctuary; they confirmed that there was no bus, so I resigned myself to a taxi. I was conscious of the cost but reminded myself that Arantzazu was a place where I definitely wanted to spend time. It was where Ignatius had prayed on his outward journey from Loyola. There, he kept a vigil and took a vow of chastity.

---

19. Sometimes the rules we invent for ourselves become a straitjacket that prevents us from actually making a good decision. Ignatius invites us to take a broader view, not making hasty decisions and ask what the greatest good would be (SE 149–55).

The taxi driver was very friendly during the one-hour drive and asked about my bandages. His name was José, or Joseba in Basque, the importance of which he impressed on me. I explained about my accident and how I was getting back on the Camino at the sanctuary. Joseba showed me some fatherly affection as he outlined my accommodation options at the sanctuary and his recommendations. I was a bit unnerved, however, when he veered off the main road to a rough concrete lane in order to bring me to the back entrance. *Trust him, trust him*, I thought, and as the vista opened up, I relaxed. The views were spectacular. From there I could appreciate the drama of the sanctuary, set high up in the Aizkorri massif, hanging precariously over the abyss amid a series of limestone summits. Joseba brought me to a *pensión* where he seemed to know everyone and where he explained to person after person my predicament (Jesuit priest, fallen on the Camino, needing to rest up). He couldn't have been more helpful and spent some time showing me around before he got my bag from the car.

After a delicious, pain-free siesta with my leg elevated, the shock of the fall, and how lucky I'd been, caught up with me. I toyed with the idea of simply abandoning the walk, but I dragged myself down to the terrace bar for a refreshment, where the view of clouds and cliffs immediately cheered me up.

I began to explore the sanctuary, getting used to walking with the knee pain. The Avant-garde basilica, angularly hewn from limestone, was built on the spot where the Virgin of Arantzazu appeared to a shepherd in 1468. I was drawn to reflect on what Ignatius had seen in that diminutive statue of the Virgin. Why had this place been so important, why had he taken the celibacy vow here—what happened during that long vigil? The statue of the Virgin was set in the wall above the main altar, dwarfed by its surroundings.

I had hoped for some quiet prayer time with the Virgin, but a huge tour group came in and bustled around in a photo frenzy. Then the sacristan, Fr. Antonio, began explaining the interior. He went through the main artists involved in the design, pointing out the details of architectural interest and relating the story of how the basilica had burned down three times. In his explanations, he confirmed that St. Ignatius had spent a whole night in vigil here and had taken a vow of chastity. When we got to see the statue of the Virgin up closer, it seemed diminutive and showed its great age. In it Mary is crowned as queen and she holds Jesus in her arms; however, it is an image of the resurrected Christ in miniature, not the usual child or dying Christ. Fr. Antonio had everyone pray for the lonely and marginalized, for broken families and all those in trouble. With everything closing for the day, I found a Franciscan priest who invited me to attend their private community Mass in the morning. Seeing my bandaged limbs, he advised me to take the next day as a day of rest. I resolved I would be obedient to his good advice.[20]

In the nearby hotel, I enjoyed the *menú del día*—a cheap, filling multicourse meal found across Spain. However, I was surprised when a whole bottle of Rioja wine appeared as part of it. I couldn't remember when I had enjoyed a meal so much. I started to feel better about things, my recovering knee, continuing the Camino again, and life in general. My hunger, fatigue, and low mood had certainly had a negative effect on me, pulling me down and affecting my decision making.[21] A strong temptation to quit the walk had dogged me all afternoon, but at dinner it seemed clear that I should continue.

---

20. Given that I had already decided to be open to hearing God through other people, it made even more sense to apply myself wholly to this sound advice, directly acting against (*agere contra*) my own impulsive inclination to keep going (SE 13, 317, 322).

21. This echoes a well-known acronym from addiction recovery wisdom: don't make a decision when hungry, angry, lonely, or tired (HALT).

The Arantzazu mountain air worked wonders. I woke up refreshed and without pain. I hobbled down to the Franciscan community, where the priest was waiting for me outside. He brought me in, explaining that they had morning prayer first, Lauds, and then Mass, but it would all be in Basque. He handed me the book of the Divine Office for reciting morning prayer and wished me good luck as he smiled, a glint in his eye. The chapel style was very simple, typical Franciscan in its use of natural wood and the color brown! The guttural Basque words echoed throughout the sanctuary, with its wood-paneled ceiling and creamy brown walls. I could see a replica of the Virgin over the celebrant's shoulder. *This must be close to what Ignatius experienced*, I thought: *the monks, the shrine, the Basque cultural experience.* The celebrant greeted me warmly after Mass. On finding out I was walking the Ignatian route, he quoted an iconic Ignatian phrase from Ignatius's autobiography: *solo y a pie*, or "alone and on foot."[22] Delighted, I explained how much it meant to me personally. Most thrilling for me was being in the footsteps of Ignatius, and in Arantzazu, the great Basque shrine, and about to continue Ignatius's route to Manresa, where he had some significant experiences and synthesized these into his *Spiritual Exercises*. I would be walking, or limping, along the ultimate pilgrimage, the Ignatian Camino, *solo y a pie*.

I trudged back up the steep hill to the *pensión* to get breakfast. The pokey dining room was empty except for one other young man. I asked to sit with him, learned that his name was Manuel and that he was walking the Ignatian Camino too—a fellow pilgrim. Our conversation got interesting when he told me he was doing a retreat based on a book he had with him. He reached into his pocket and took out

---

22. Ignatius is captured in this iconic phrase, "*solo y a pie* (alone and on foot)," to describe his journey as a personal search for God. Brian Grogan, *Alone and on Foot: Ignatius of Loyola* (Dublin: Veritas, 2009).

a Spanish version of Ignatius's *Spiritual Exercises* combined with his autobiography! I was taken aback and overcome by a feeling of providence at work. Unaware of my vocation as a Jesuit priest and spiritual director, and of how central this book was to my Jesuit training and to my work helping people recognize the signs of God's actions in their life, Manuel explained that he had bought the book during a retreat program and was trying to work his way through it on his own. He was finding it very tough and felt that he was getting nowhere with it.

Manuel was a young Basque man who worked as a secondary school teacher. Even though he came from a big family, he had lost touch with them and lived alone. Having been through a number of difficult situations of grief and being let down by others, he was trying to put his life back together again and was exploring spirituality. He had been to several parish events and prayer meetings, but he was looking for something more meaningful to him. He was attracted to St. Ignatius as a fellow Basque and from what he had read about him online. Manuel was planning to walk the Ignatian Camino as a ten-day retreat, and when he was doing research before his trip, the Spiritual Exercises *was the one key text that he kept coming across.*

I explained to Manuel that I was a Jesuit priest and that leading people through this book was part of my job. As I talked with Manuel, I felt God asking me something through that conversation. I explained to him how the *Spiritual Exercises* was meant for spiritual directors, not people making the retreat: almost like how a book on automobiles might help mechanics more than everyday drivers. I listened to him talk about his life and how he hoped to heal some personal issues, and how the initial Exercises had confused him. I realized that I had one chance to give him some guidance, as he was leaving after breakfast. Thinking on my feet, I asked him to pass me the book, and I showed him the Examen, a five-step prayer and review of the day that allows us to look at our life through God's eyes so that we're able to notice the gifts and blessings of the day.[23] I shared with him some practical advice about staying in gratitude, not just focusing on our individual failings, and also looking at the variety of feelings we all have in one day. At that point I became aware of other diners stopping to listen.

I explained in my best Spanish about Ignatius's discernment of different moods and how he learned that this was God working within his experience. I showed Manuel the part in the autobiography about the discernment of spirits.[24] I used the example of how I fell and tried futilely to keep walking. I reflected that this compulsion was not good (this internal opposition to a life-enhancing decision is defined as *desolation*), and I had decided to get medical help, which had led to taking a day off.[25] This decision had brought me back to *consolation*, defined as living in the truth of the situation, rejecting negative compulsions, and experiencing some measure of inner peace. The consolation I was feeling, a humble acceptance of the situation, was what I believe God wanted. In the same way, I assured Manuel that God was working with him, communicating with him continually. The signs of God were always there, I told him, and the Examen would help him tune in to them. Faith was something you worked

---

23. For guidance on the Examen, see SE 43.

24. Imagining different lifestyles, such as imitating St. Francis or winning the hand of a lady, left a distinct emotional or affective aftereffect. Ignatius discovered that one led toward God (consolation) and the other way from God (desolation). Joseph N. Tylenda, SJ, *A Pilgrim's Journey: The Autobiography of Ignatius of Loyola* (Collegeville, MN: Liturgical Press, 1991), No. 8, p. 14.

25. Ignatius defined *consolation* and *desolation*, these inner movements or moods, as the way God works within us to draw us in certain life-giving directions and away from others. *Consolation* is defined as a movement toward light and love. It is accompanied by a deep-down peace that comes from our living life in a Christlike way, acting with courage, mercy, and kindness. *Consolation* opens us up to the world, new possibilities, and other people (SE 316). *Desolation* is just the opposite. Though it can feature superficial delight, it often features a deeper unease. *Desolation* is an experience of being out of tune with the Spirit, turned in on oneself, and isolated. In a positive sense, *desolation* is a sign of God's intervening to stir us into action and reform (SE 316, 317).

out on your feet in ordinary experience, not something extraordinary to work out in your head. I felt such great compassion for him on his personal journey and assured him that God also felt endless compassion for him. I fondly wished Manuel a *buen camino*, or good walk, and watched him from the door as he set off and wound his way down the trail.

With a day still to fill, I decided to explore the rest of the shrine. I found one isolated building intriguingly labelled Misterio, or "mystery," on the side of the hill on its own. It was a low concrete building, designed as a sanctuary or retreat with huge glass windows. The entrance was hacked out of the exposed limestone rock, which was startlingly physical and natural, especially one corner where the water was weeping from a small recess in the rock's face that had plants growing in it. The next room had a dramatic view of sheer white cliffs over the valley, framed by several hawthorn bushes (from which Arantzazu takes its name). I found a seat there and let the music playing in the background captivate me as I enjoyed imagining myself transported across the landscape, sky, and foliage.[26] The roaring wind reminded me of the Holy Spirit at Pentecost, and I remembered the Hebrew word for wind, *ruah*, which refers to the renewing power of God's love that blows where it wills. *What new chapter or adventure am I embarking on? How is the Spirit working through all this?* I wondered. In the valley I could see a huge bird soar on the thermal lift, and I knew from Joseba, the taxi driver from the day before, that it was probably a vulture. The bird's grace made for compulsive viewing. In this place, I understood anew the word *sanctuary* to mean a place of safety and refuge, and I knew this place would have spoken to the newly converted Ignatius. He would have found space, advice, and the inspiration to leave his old life behind and tune in more to

---

26. The music was reminiscent of the track "Sanctuary" on the 1997 album *White Stones* by Secret Garden.

what the immanent God was doing in his life. I was likewise in need of sanctuary, time out from the hectic schedule of bereavement talks and retreats back home that were exacting a certain toll.

On the way back down the hill, I dropped into the basilica for what would be my last visit since I was leaving Arantzazu the next morning. I sat there praying for inspiration and specifically for the same inspiration Ignatius had received in this place so many years before. I had a very strong desire to go to confession, as I imagined Ignatius might have done here to reinforce his commitment to seek God in his life. After waiting in line for twenty minutes, I was thinking of leaving. Then I remembered how clear the insight had been to do the confession in the first place. I reinforced my patience and penitential attitude, all the stronger for the wait. The priest invited me to sit beside him on the bench and we began to talk. His kind and compassionate attitude helped me, as did his insistence that I let the past be the past. Appropriately, he gave me three Hail Marys to pray as penance. Praying alone afterward, I felt lighter, and closer to Ignatius. My leg felt much better and all seemed well for the next day's departure.

4

MISTY MOUNTAIN HOP

Up early for what was likely to be a challenging day in the mountains, I prayed silently for safety and security: *"My God is my rock, in whom I find protection, my shield, the power that saves me, and my place of safety."* The words from Psalm 18 really spoke to me about facing the fear of the unknown and protection against whatever dangers might come.[27] As I walked out of the *pensión* with all my gear, a young man came after me, saying he had overheard me the night before mention I was walking the Ignatian Camino. He introduced himself as Xavier and invited me back inside to introduce me to his slightly older, wiry friend Iñigo. They were having breakfast and told me they had met in a local hiking club. Xavier worked in landscaping and Iñigo in computers. Xavier and I hit it off right away, as we were both interested in Ignatius of Loyola and were committed pilgrims on this Ignatian trail. Xavier explained that he was only able to do short stints on the Camino, as long breaks made maintaining and reentering the world of work very difficult. He added that it was especially difficult to bring the Camino feeling back into everyday life, which is a common complaint. I sympathized, explaining that my cuts and bruises, acquired while setting out on the Camino, had, ironically, afforded

---

27. Prayer is about asking for what you want, your deeper desires, not the superficial ones, and keeping it "real" above all else (SE 48).

me the great opportunity for humility—making me rely on the kindness of others and forcing me to trust in providence. Conscious of time, I bid Xavier and Iñigo farewell and set out, knowing that they were sure to catch up with me on the trail later.

The gravel trail leaving from Arantzazu snaked up steeply into the misty mountains. I had to accept a growing unease about whether I was able to manage it, whether my leg would hold up or I would get stuck up on the mountain. As an experienced leader of walks in Ireland, and having survived some hair-raising hikes in Poland and Canada, too, I normally wouldn't have thought twice about heading up a mountain alone. I reassured myself that a good start is always half the battle, that the doctor had given me the all-clear, and that I could stop at any time. The reasonable fear of further injury was something I had to acknowledge but also pray with and work through.

The rocky Aizkorri-Aratz Natural Park enveloped me as I creaked cold, stiff, and sore up the gravel path. Looking down, all I could see were my white bandages, skinny walking sticks, and labored knee movements. Focusing my attention outward, I saw lots of sinkholes: a sure sign of limestone rock, rivers, and caverns, just like my home, County Fermanagh, in Ireland. It was beautiful in an eerie way, with the mist and deep shadows frayed by the wind. I had several flashbacks to *The Lord of the Rings*, a book I had loved as a teenager for its epic struggle between good and evil. I could imagine Ignatius here reflecting on similar spiritual forces that acted on the human soul—darkness and light, pulling in opposite directions, fighting for superiority like whispers on the wind. My discernment was helping me to separate genuine attractions to the good from seductive temptations to evil, a vivid reminder for me to walk in the light and avoid the dark by keeping to the path. The somber, silent surroundings, the craggy outcrops, and the squat boulders nestling under beech thickets gave off a timeless and slightly sinister air. Then, unseen birds broke the silence with the purest birdsong that made my heart sing. It gave me courage that I would make it, despite my need to limp along, the feeling taking away a lot of doubt and affirming my decision to walk.[28] I was glad to be alive, to see such beauty that I wouldn't have thought possible twenty-four hours earlier.

As I gained altitude, it slowly dawned on me that I was feeling a great inner freedom.[29] The fall and subsequent fear about getting back on the trail had led me to hand this whole thing over to God, forcing me to lower my own expectations and to commit myself to continue as best I could. I couldn't go on being dictated to by fear and anxiety. These emotions had their place, but I knew they could be very bad counselors, too.[30] I thought to myself, *If I give in now, then I might as well be on my journey home. That would be safe and predictable. But oh, this beautiful day! Every step I take is a bonus, and I am grateful for every moment on this providential path.* This experience brought me into the present moment, I had no expectations, and each step brought me closer to reaching the top of the mountain pass. I refused to listen to the insistent voice reminding me I'd have to descend the path too. I concentrated instead on my steps, for it was very rough underfoot. An exercise in mindfulness, I placed my walking stick, one foot, the other stick, and then the other foot. On and on, slowly and rhythmically, I was climbing a mountain of fear.

---

28. Ignatius says that a sense of peacefulness or rightness about a decision amounts to a confirmation or clarity about an often difficult choice (SE 183).

29. Inner freedom is that delicate balance of facing our fears, acting against negative influences, and making the best decision possible in less-than-ideal circumstances (SE 149–55). Here the tension was between immobility and recuperation (the safe option) and cautious walking forward (the adventurous option).

30. Separating out biases, strong emotions, and unhelpful tendencies is often the biggest challenge in discernment. Even though Ignatius places a strong emphasis on feelings in the Spiritual Exercises, he also builds in cognitive or rational checks too. Michael J. O'Sullivan, SJ, "Trust Your Feelings, but Use Your Head: Discernment and the Psychology of Decision Making," *Studies in the Spirituality of Jesuits* 22, no. 4 (1990): 1–41.

Eventually the incline decreased, the walking was easier, and as I passed through a long tunnel of ash trees, I heard a discordant tinkling of bells. Intrigued, I carved a path through the long grass and threaded my way through the rampart of rocky buttresses. Ethereal in the mist was a tall, imperious, shaggy sheep eyeing me curiously. Abruptly, it went back to graze with the rest of the flock. There must have been over 200 in all, each with a bell producing a slightly different tone. Faced with this chaotic but pleasant animal orchestra, I forgot about my troubles. After some time, I carefully picked my way back down through the slippery rock, happy to have experienced this melodic mystery in this remote, foggy place.

Soon after, the path had flattened out, and I guessed I was at the top. The quaint Urbia hermitage emerged from the silent mist, ringed with pruned sycamore trees standing guard all around this stone chapel. I tried the doors, but they were locked and the windows shuttered. The splendid isolation was illusory, though, as 900 feet beyond the hermitage, I came across a combined bar, restaurant, and *pensión*. Inside, people were seated and the bartender at work. I was welcomed in by a huge wood stove radiating wonderful heat. The warmth inside reminded me of how cold it actually was outside, 41 degrees with the wind chill. Given that we were at an altitude of 3,500 feet, it was not that surprising.

As I sat enjoying my favorite treat, *café con leche* and a *torta*, I looked around the rough stone bar with minimal furniture. There was one man standing at the bar and another two sitting in the corner near the woodstove. I asked if I could join them, more to keep near the fire than to have company. They were very friendly and spoke *castellano* with thick Basque accents. They told me that the guy at the bar was a real shepherd, complete with sheepdogs tied up outside. I rushed after him as he left, just to say hello, but my romantic bubble was burst as he stepped into a Toyota Hilux pickup truck and rocketed down the dirt road. The dogs, meanwhile, under his instructions, had set about clearing the nearby hill of sheep. The fog was lifting to reveal a completely different day and landscape. I gave thanks for having made it this far. Up to this point, I had seen trees, rock tunnels, and oppressive fog, but in front of me then rose interlocking hills and grassy slopes with jagged peaks in the distance.

Back in the bar, I was left with one very entertaining guy. He really had it in for the Jesuits and teased me unmercifully. For a respite, I went to the bar for a second coffee. When I got back to the table, getting tired of the teasing, I resolved to ask this guy what he was really about. He worked as a car mechanic. I could see the toil written on his hands. He told me he was single. A faraway look came into his eyes when he said that, which made me think there was loneliness there. He told me he walked the mountains on his own a lot, didn't like being away from home, and was a regular at the bar. Then, he reminded me that I had been there for an hour and a half. I first found this man annoying, but it turned out that talking with him and soaking up the warmth of the stove made me totally forget about the trail. It was a welcome reprieve after all. The music changed in that moment from a Basque folk group called Oskorri to the familiar drone of the Ramones. I took it as a cue to get going.

I set off down a broad valley with glittering limestone peaks all around. Being able to see the horizon took away any focus I had on my problems and placed me in this beautiful natural park, a stunning high-country walk by any standard. Evidence this was sheep country was everywhere, with the telltale close-cropped grass and droppings all over the place. In the distance, herds dotted the mountain slopes. I came across ramshackle little stone houses built by shepherds, many of which had makeshift sheep pens, and some had groups of sheep squeezed in tight. The road had turned to gravel and was deeply pitted by recent rains. I stopped to take a stone out of my shoe and thought, *This is a good philosophy for dealing with problems in general, not letting them develop.* I thought of the limestone sinkholes that I had seen earlier: like any corroding reality, they needed to be tackled early on, while still manageable; otherwise they could swallow you up, along with your well-being and stability.

I exited the forest with a slight limp, my knee giving trouble, and entered a clearing scattered with brown and white horses. Grazing peacefully, they were oblivious to my presence, and I feasted on the scene. Now after noon, there was still no sign of Xavier or Iñigo, the two Basque hikers I had met earlier that morning, but I trusted in their imminent arrival, and this gave me feelings of great security.

I stopped for lunch in a beech thicket with a view out over an immense valley toward Vitoria-Gasteiz and reflected on how the day had turned out for the better, how worried I had been initially, how I had stepped out of the fog of fear and anxiety and into a stunning Basque mountain landscape. I had a sense of being on track and of fully shaking off my injury within a day or two. Part of me was sorry to be coming down out of the mountains, into civilization, and out of that magical place. Turning off the app, I resolved to enjoy the view and savor the nourishment of my lunch, which, like everything done in the outdoor air, tasted exquisite.

Back on the rough track, I went gingerly downhill, and the walking sticks came in handy as a kind of brake. I remembered the advice I'd been given once: descending a mountain is at least as much work as ascending. This is when accidents often happen: you expect to coast downhill so you stop concentrating, and that leads to mistakes. Eventually, the track wound its way out the other flank of the mountain, and my destination, Araia, came into view, looking deceptively close. Unexpectedly, I caught up with my two Basque friends from that morning, who had stopped at a crossroads. They must have overtaken me when I stepped off the path to eat. The problem was that we were now all lost, having missed a turn on the descent off the mountain. I had mentally switched off as had they. I quickly checked my phone app, which indicated that we were five miles off the track. The other two were convinced they had figured out a way to rejoin the trail. They wanted to go back uphill a ways, but my app pointed the opposite direction. I trusted my app, even though the trail it indicated was faint and lacking signage, but they were convinced the other way was better. Choosing humility over arrogance, I merely presented the evidence from my phone and left it up to them to decide. Fortunately, they agreed on the route on my app because it brought us down from the mountain. I reflected on how easy it was to get lost, how hard it is to make decisions in a group, and how to determine what is sound advice. Navigation in the mountains is like navigation in everyday life: decisions have consequences, and it's worth taking time over them.

With the day's destination in sight and the rocky path steeply inclined, my two trail mates began to speed up. I struggled to keep up. To go faster, I also found myself taking more risks and being careless about my steps. Remembering the events that led to my fall, I wondered why I was making such an effort, sacrificing my well-being for the feeling of security of having company. I was acutely conscious that I did not want to be out alone in the vast woods with a gamey leg. However, I also knew that I had to stop, face my fears, slow down, and go on alone.[31] When we came back onto the main Camino trail, I bade them farewell and felt the bliss and freedom of rest as I sank into a ditch. In that sun-filtered glade it struck me that I was alone but happy despite the pain and struggle. The peace eventually sank

---

31. The trade-off was between security and support versus acknowledging the increasing pain and need for rest. Here, the need for security became an "attachment," hindering the process of slowing down and alleviating the pain (SE 149–55).

into my bones as I knew I had made the right decision to hang back and listen to my body.[32]

Much later, arriving into Araia, I was totally beat—everything hurt, especially my knee, and the soles of my feet burned. At a *pensión* on the outskirts of town, I asked for a room, but it was full. Stumbling into town, I came across a cyclist. I asked him about a room, and he told me that another *pensión* was back up the hill I had just come down. Reluctantly backtracking, I followed him to a family home beside the road. He called in through the high garden fence to a woman working at the back. Out came this vivacious woman, tanned and radiating health. Named Eguskina (which means "sunshine" in Basque), she was the epitome of kindness and warmth. She showed me into a lovely room of light and pastel colors and told me about a drama festival happening in town later that night. To my amazement, she mentioned that a hiker, Manuel, had been there the night before and had told her to expect me, the priest with the bandages and bruises—I hadn't been too difficult to spot! She said that Manuel had arrived equally low and dispirited the night before and she had tried to cheer him up. She also told me about how she always tried to make people feel welcome, and I assured her of the great impact this had on me, of how it makes such a difference when you are feeling low and done in. I felt like Eguskina's vocation was there, where she used conversation and positivity to make a difference to the visitors who came to her home.

Eguskina had stayed local to look after her elderly mother, and she raised her family of three children in this small Basque town where everyone knew one another. She had studied physiotherapy in college, but, unable to find a full-time job, had decided to rent out rooms and teach exercise classes at night. Eguskina didn't identify as a practicing Catholic, but she

---

32. Consolation or peace returns after taking time to rest, affirming this decision and opening up new possibilities (SE 183, 188).

was sympathetic to all things spiritual and employed some meditation techniques. From her own large Basque family, she knew the importance of hospitality and welcoming people, of doing ordinary things extraordinarily well. She had lived in Paris for some years previously and found it a very lonely place. From that experience, she had resolved to always welcome the stranger in her life. She reminded me of the famous Basque Jesuit, Francisco Gárate—every time he opened the university door, he treated each visitor with respect worthy of Christ himself.

On Eguskina's recommendation, I went to the evening Mass in the eighteenth-century sandstone Andra Mari (Our Lady) hermitage on the hill and sat in on the rosary, which, recited in Basque, was enchanting. The Baroque *retablo* over the altar was dotted with scallop shells, and there was a Saint James cross carved above the door. This reminded me that this had been an important stop on the medieval Camino de Santiago route. After the rosary recitation, I found the priest, Eduardo, in the hermitage's simple sacristy. Even though there were no spare vestments for me to concelebrate, Eduardo had me sit at his side during Mass. There was something moving about the utter simplicity of the sacristy. It was an invitation to break bread with Christ himself; his self-sacrificing love for me was palpable in the gestures and words. As I listened to the Spanish words, I was transported to the road to Emmaus, where I walked along and only recognized Christ—tangible, concrete, powerfully present—in the breaking of the bread.[33]

After Mass I had a great meal of *tortilla vasca*, a Basque omelet, and a large slice of almond cake. Then, I wandered down to the town square where a group of acrobats were entertaining the crowds at the drama festival. I was happy to bump into Xavier, and asking after Iñigo, I learned that they were staying in the same *pensión*. Xavier settled into conversation and we found out that we had a lot in common, especially on spiritual topics. He asked if I knew Taizé, France,

---

33. For Ignatius, the Eucharist was the greatest sign of Christ's love (SE 298, 303).

a place close to my heart where I first learned about pilgrimage and met the inspirational founder of that community, Br. Roger.[34] Xavier and I reminisced about "the church with no walls," where everyone sits on the ground and the chants enter your soul.

When I prayed the Examen[35] later that evening, reflecting over my day, I was grateful for all the heartwarming moments of insight, the stunning nature, and the pleasant people I had met along the way. I also reflected on what a good decision it was earlier to slow down and let Xavier and Iñigo go ahead, to protect myself and go at my own pace. Those changes were marked in my mood and helped lessen the pain. I felt, too, that although I made it through the mountains successfully that day, it had been perhaps a bit too much walking for my condition. A few miles less would have been more suitable. I decided to take things easier the next day to give my knee time to heal. I needed to find the balance between a healthy workout and overstressing my body. Ignatius might have recognized this tension, this balance. After all, he himself limped around these mountains on his way to spiritual freedom and a new life. I drifted off to sleep thinking, *I have nothing to worry about.*

34. Founded in 1940, the Taizé community is an ecumenical Christian monastic community in Taizé, France. It is composed of brothers, from Catholic and Protestant traditions, from about thirty countries across the world, who largely minister to young people. For more information, see the community's website at www.taize.fr/en.

35. Known as the Examen of Consciousness, this prayer is central in Ignatius's Spiritual Exercises (SE 43), because it helps you process the day and reflect on the lights and shadows in your daily life (see www.loyolapress.com/how-can-i-pray-try-the-daily-examen.html).

5
COLD MOUNTAIN MUD

Early morning saw me limp out of Araia village while only a handful of locals moved around in the murky dawn hours. I was looking forward to an easier day than the one before. However, I knew from my Ignatian Camino guide that on this day's trek, after crossing the valley, I would ascend into the Entzia Mountains, through the San Román Mountain Pass. To reach the pass, I would have to ascend "only" 1,600 feet, but that didn't sound too gentle to me. I knew my knee was improving, but the weather wasn't. It was another dull day with mist shrouding the surrounding mountains—pretty from afar, but it meant damp, drizzle, and cold on the mountain. I was grateful to be able to walk, something I wouldn't take for granted. I resolved to make the best of whatever this day promised, so I placed the day in the hands of the Lord and trusted that whatever was to come, I would be able for it.[36]

Initially, gravel tracks through open farmland made the going easy, and my eyes were elevated to the rocky rim all around. Atop one craggy ridge, I made out a metal cross above the mist, forlorn and spectral, like Golgotha itself.

To get to the village of San Román, I had to cross the tracks of the main railway line. I scampered across the glistening rails as if I were in

---

36. This is a prayer of desire, wanting to hand over the entire day to God (SE 24).

mortal danger. As I climbed onto the platform, there was a huge sign with an arrow to "Irun," the starting place of the Camino de Santiago, my previous pilgrimage four years before. Nostalgic, I tried not to make comparisons with an idealized past; doing so undermined the present. I had to shrug off the temptation to compare. If I started to compare this walk with a previous one, or even myself with other people, I would easily despair. This moment had to be lived as an entirely new and different experience, with its own challenges and joys.

The trail began to wind its way up into the Entzia Mountains, ascending into the mist. The surroundings gradually disappeared, and I found myself in a sunken track threaded through by a faint path of slick stones. I was alone, on foot, and cold. The recurring thought about the lunacy of this endeavor crossed my mind, but I went back to the fundamentals: *I will get through this tough, uphill section, and it will be great.* Every so often the mist-shrouded track would open up for a tantalizing glimpse of fields with grazing sheep, indifferent to the blinding fog. Eventually, the path itself was so muddy that there was no way around. I had to wade right through it. *It's just wet earth,* I told myself, *water, clay, and organic matter. The stuff I am made of!* I squelched and slid on. At a stile on the trail, I met a Spanish hiker coming the opposite way who was happy to exchange pleasantries, but, like me, keen to get back to his silent business through the mist. There was a peculiar magic to being out in moisture-soaked nature. Hours flew by with no recognizable sign of progress, except the occasional Camino signpost.

At times the path disappeared completely, muddy fields took over, and I continued carefully, trying to avoid getting lost. I was so grateful for the navigation app on my phone. I had to resort to it now and again (even though I blamed it for my accident!). Even in the absence of visible signs or landmarks, it would always indicate the correct path, as I had learned earlier. I marveled at it and certainly benefited greatly from its use.[37] Without it I would have been totally lost and potentially in real trouble. With it, however, I could have an exhilarating adventure and feel achievement every time I saw a Camino sign, feeling reassured that I didn't really need them.

I began seeing lots of snails in my path. They were out enjoying the wet wonderland. They seemed to signal to me the gift of slow progress: taking the sure and safe route instead of a risky one and trusting in arriving at your destination on your own time. Like a Camino snail, I was carrying my house on my back, taking my time, and contentedly resigned to a slow and steady progress.

As the path crested a forested ridge, there was a large animal parked right in my path. As I got closer, I could tell it was bovine, and, ominously, it had horns. I edged closer to look for the anatomy between its hind legs: male or female. Fortunately for me, it was female. The huge, docile Charolais cow moved out of the way. I could see that she had a cowbell and then heard other cattle clanking and stirring among the trees. I was drawn back to memories of being brought up on the family farm, how I hadn't enjoyed it as a teenager but now treasured the bucolic memories and all the useful, lifesaving knowledge. We had a chunky Charolais bull that, when crossed with our tiny Hereford cows, made for very difficult calving. We used to watch the cows closely and assist at the calving, often by having to pull out the calf. It was a stressful job, but nothing matched the wonder of seeing a spindly newborn calf take its first steps. *Often, really good things come out of very difficult moments*, I told myself, convinced that this difficult walk would also bring good into my life.

---

37. An Ignatian view sees technology and the world as a gift that can help us get closer to God, when used discerningly, as a means rather than an end (SE 23). Brendan McManus, SJ, "The Jesuit Smartphone," www.jesuit.ie/blog/brendan-mcmanus/the-jesuit-smartphone/.

The previous crest turned out to be a false summit, and the still-ascending path turned into a sea of creamy mud that clung to my boots, making my feet heavy and slippery. There was no way around the quagmires, and not wanting to turn back, I had to go straight through them. In some places, someone with a tractor had attempted to scrape the mud to one side and fill in the path with gravel. The result was patchy at best, and the effort was probably futile. It was impossible to stop the encroaching sludge, which was fueled by abundant moisture and loose earth. Eventually, I gave up trying to pick my way across islands of dry grass or save my clothes. I figured the mud wouldn't kill me, and the best way through was simply to jump in and enjoy it. Wading in mud reminded me of the childish joy of splashing through puddles with full abandon, of embracing the messiness of life and going with the flow.[38]

Around noon, I came upon a cold upland forest. The mist was still in full effect. The beech trees, encased in a woolly moss, dripped water onto the leaf and bracken carpet underneath. The scene was eerily silent and majestic; I was enclosed in a cocoon of fog that excluded the world. Wearing only shorts and a T-shirt, I put on my waterproof poncho to keep dry. Like most Camino gear, it was performing a double duty, keeping me warm and also dry. For lunch, I found a convenient mossy rock, wrapped my rain poncho around myself, and sat down to eat. Rest after effort, relief after pain, and food after hunger made for a lovely meal. Out of the mist emerged a couple engaged in conversation. They were so engrossed with each other that they passed by without seeing me even though I was only 25 yards away. Of course, I was camouflaged, dressed in dark green and sitting under a tree, but I was convinced it was magic! Delighted with my new invisibility, I let them go on their way. I imagined that

---

38. God is with us in the mess, helping us through difficult times. Jim Deeds and Brendan McManus, SJ, *Finding God in the Mess* (Chicago: Loyola Press, 2020).

I had become so much at one with nature that I had disappeared into it. *How would it be to live here, through the cycles of the seasons, watching things decay and come back to life?* I wondered. A shiver brought me back to reality. I was alone, in the woods, and still had miles to go to my destination.

The path started to wind its way down from the San Román Mountain Pass. My knee really began to hurt on the way down, so I went along gingerly. My navigation app had proved invaluable that day already, but even so I stopped to ask a friendly farmer for directions. The human interaction provided some much-needed warmth after the cold morning in the mountains. When he discovered I could converse in Spanish, he took the opportunity to point out some megalithic features nearby. He told me about monoliths and dolmens that revealed ancient farming practices. Eventually, he pointed me to the right path and told me I only had three and a half miles left—much farther than I had thought! Sapped by the cold and the heavy going, I took a break to replenish my body and spirit for the last few miles.

Fortunately, the scenery of the Arana valley, which had opened up before me, distracted me entirely. After a morning encased in mud and mist, I walked along an unusual cream-colored gravel path that curved serpentine-like between fields of cut barley that were speckled with golden bales. It lifted my heart to see the entire valley clearly—an ordered, symmetrical weave of fields, hedges, and harvest, all surrounded by mountains. I focused in on my apparent destination; I was close. Even though the signpost said one and a half miles, it looked more like just one. I needed it to be close. Summoning the last of my strength, I plowed on through the pain and fatigue, refreshed by thoughts of food, drink, and sleep.

As I hit the outskirts of the small town, the first building I came across was a white sandstone church. Not wanting to pass up the opportunity to visit it, I pulled myself up the steep steps to the raised rock platform where the old church stood. I entered and met a woman who was busy looking after the place with a watering can in her hand. The scent of fresh flowers was pervasive and invited meditation. She told me that I was in the Hermitage of Andra María (Our Lady) in Ullibarri, a little more than a mile short of where I expected to be. She began to lock up, and I realized I still had some distance to walk, the last miles being the longest. She very kindly gave me directions and accompanied me to the main street to point out the way. Dispirited, I decided to stop for a pick-me-up at the local pub. When I walked into the bar, most of the many people inside turned to look at me. I must have cut quite a figure, red faced with exertion, legs covered with scrapes and scabs, and my boots covered in mud. They cleared a way to the bar for me so I could order. I took my drink outside, away from the noise, and mulled over what had been a challenging day.

Picking up my backpack and getting my body going again caused me to grit my teeth. The trail went up a hill and across some country to the next town, but I figured it would be faster to walk along the main road. A taxi whizzed past me, and I desperately wished for a moment that I was sitting in the back seat. Then, it started to rain. I forged ahead regardless, unwilling to face the bother of putting on my rain gear again. I felt free, though, and a real pilgrim despite everything.

At last, I could see the Alda *pensión* from a long way off. I prayed there was a room available. I certainly couldn't face walking on to the next town. I had committed to the Camino ideal of not booking ahead, but here I was questioning the wisdom of "trusting in providence."[39] When I arrived at the front door, a woman spoke to me from a window high above, asking me about the walk and how it had gone. I filled her in on a day of rain, mud, and general grit. She had

---

39. A key part of Jesuit training is the walking pilgrimage, normally undertaken without money, to learn reliance entirely on God alone as Ignatius himself had done. *Constitutions of the Society of Jesus*, no. 67.

a room, and a feeling of overwhelming gratitude flooded my being! I couldn't quite hear the price she quoted me, but at that moment, I was just glad I would be able to put down the leaden backpack, wash my muddy feet, and sink into a mattress for the evening.

My two Basque friends, Xavier and Iñigo, had again overtaken me and were already settled in. I walked into my room, shed my gear, sank into the bed, and lay there gratefully pain-free. I was almost unconscious but too exhausted to sleep or move. I just lay there, in a half-dead sleep, unaware of my surroundings, until a bell rang for dinner. I was so thankful for this basic accommodation: room and board, the two things I needed most.

It was good to see my two Basque friends at dinner. The meal was simple but good, and many of the ingredients were from the family's own garden. We enjoyed spicy sausage and bread, followed by a huge salad of olives, egg, lettuce, tomato, and onion. We ate in a comfortable silence, too tired to talk, just enjoying the food and the simple surroundings. Another plate of home-cured bacon strips and potato chips was equally welcomed. Dessert was a bowl of fruit: apples, oranges, and peaches. We saved what was left for the next day's walk.

Reenergized by the food, the three of us went for a walk around the tiny village. It only took a few minutes to see everything, but we did discover a bar that was open. It had nothing outside to advertise itself, but one of my companions heard voices within. It was very simple: a cement floor, freshly plastered white walls, and harsh strip lighting. But it did offer the essentials. Perhaps influenced by the simple setting, we ordered just two coffees and a fizzy lemon.

Hearing my friends' Basque accents, the bartender started chatting with them rapidly and animatedly. I couldn't keep up and quickly was out of the conversation. Their body language reinforced this, and the bartender stood with his hands extended in front of my two friends in a perfect triangle. I felt irritated and excluded. I wondered if it was my injury that made me react like this. I made several attempts to break into the conversation, but the bartender wasn't having any of it, and my friends didn't seem to notice. It feels horrible to be excluded, and I sat sulking on my phone as a sign of protest.

My evening was going downhill, and I desperately wanted to rescue it. Though I was unaware of it, the others had announced in Basque that I was a Jesuit. As a result, Mikael, who was married to a local and who had arrived in the bar earlier, came over to introduce himself as a Jesuit alumnus. As we animatedly spoke about all things Jesuit, I started to feel better, a connection made in this unfamiliar place. With new energy, I thought about some way I could bring everyone together. I knew Xavier liked to sing, so I asked him if the bartender would let us sing a few songs. The bartender was only too happy to oblige; he was also a singer, who sang regularly in a choir. And suddenly he and Xavier launched into some lovely Basque songs, complete with harmonies. I didn't know what they were singing about, but from the emotional tone, I thought I could distinguish themes of love and heartbreak, freedom and oppression. It came to my turn, and with Xavier Googling the lyrics, we sang "The Wild Rover" and "Molly Malone." Others joined in, with more and more Basque songs finding expression. With the songs still ringing in my head, I went home early but happy. I was grateful to Mikael especially, for intervening and helping dig me out of some desolation. I found myself happily humming Jack White's version of the old American folk song "The Wayfaring Stranger."

Mikael attended a Jesuit school in Bilbao, Spain. A graduate from the 1990s, Mikael was a gregarious, kindhearted giant of a man who spoke fondly of his alma mater. He still meets with his old classmates monthly, enjoying the company of his lifelong friends and reminiscing on their school days. At one time he was discerning a vocation to the Jesuits, but eventually he decided to get married instead. He has three young children. After several jobs in the social sector, he joined the Jesuit Refugee Service, which was founded by the Jesuit brother from the Basque Country, Pedro Arrupe, SJ, a great inspiration. Mikael believed in hospitality, making people feel at home, and he accepted and welcomed refugees and asylum seekers by supporting Jesuit Refugee Service centers across Europe. Based in Malta, Mikael was on the Camino with his family. He was passionate about the refugee crisis in southern Spain and along the Mediterranean. With typical Basque intensity, he spoke with great personal conviction and commitment.

As I walked up the town's main street, I heard a car horn sounding behind me. I thought it was odd to make so much noise at that hour. Then, as it got closer, I saw it was a minibus of sorts, lit from within. Then it dawned on me: it was an ice cream van, out at this late hour in this little town in the mountains. I had to support this guy and asked for a cone. I opted for vanilla, a safe bet all over the world and a real treat. Back in my cool, russet-colored room, I prayed the Examen, reviewing my day. My moment of invisibility under the tree sprung to mind, such a moment of consolation in a muddy, strenuous day. Also remarkable was the change in my mood in the bar from feeling isolated to animating the singing, a change facilitated by Mikael and establishing a human connection.[40] As I lay down to rest, I noticed my knee was still bothering me. *Surely it should be better by now*, I thought. I considered walking only half the normal distance the next day.

---

40. When emotions of negativity and desolation isolate us, we must find a way to act against them. Known as *agere contra* in Latin, positive steps to get back on track and into consolation are described by Ignatius (SE 13, 317, 322).

6

THE HARD ROAD

It felt as if I had closed my eyes for just a few seconds; then, suddenly, it was morning. Sluggish to get going, I threw my things together and dragged myself out early onto the gravel road. My reward was a low sun streaming from under the clouds, revealing every contour of the Arana valley corridor. To the right, high cliffs and serrated edges dominated, and above them, dark clouds threatened. The rough road cut a straight line through fields of corn and potatoes. My elongated shadow stretched down the road in front of me, reminding me of my time on the Camino de Santiago years ago. My knee was feeling okay again, and I resolved to walk the whole stage. *This is where it all begins*, I thought. *I will shake off this injury and get down to some serious walking!*

A few minutes later, shots rang out. I presumed it was farmers scaring off birds, but as I got closer, I could see a number of hunters firing their guns in the fields below me. The hunting season for pigeon, partridge, and woodcock had just opened. It felt a bit unnerving to be so near birds being shot out of the sky. The hunters had great accuracy and the birds were snatched up by waiting dogs. Spooked, I accelerated past them making myself as tall and noticeable as possible.

Walking slowly through this fertile valley was a real pleasure and easily lent itself to meditation.[41] My two Basque friends caught up, and we fell into step together. The trail left the road, becoming a rough cart track winding through some sheep paddocks and then plunging into a ravine. At that point, my knee started to hurt again, and I was caught in the same bind as before, trying to keep up. Xavier and Iñigo were gracious, waiting for me, but all the enjoyment went out of the walk. The terrain was challenging, largely off road, and without any chance of a ride with a passing vehicle. As we came out of a forest on a downhill stretch of road, Iñigo, who was walking behind me, commented on my worsening limp. Hearing this confirmation from another person was helpful. It was difficult for me to accept that there was a problem as I couldn't see it clearly and was heavily invested in continuing.[42]

Though I was trying to convince myself it was improving, the knee was very painful. The only option I had was to stop walking at this pace; I resolved that once we reached the next village, I would let the other two go on ahead.

A red-roofed church poked up from behind the next hill, a huge relief. A farmer on a tractor passed us with a bale of hay on the front loader. I dreamed of being carried along in that hay above the hard road. We came to a small hermitage above the village, and I was determined not to pass up a church. A woman carrying a basket of fruit told us where to find the church warden next door. José Maria was smoking a large cigar at his window and agreed to open the chapel for

---

41. The world and everything in it, including ourselves, has been created by God. God is continually trying to reach us and communicate with us, and our role is to be open and receptive (SE 23, 235–37).
42. Discernment, or good decision making, is about overcoming personal bias and attachments to become more objective and free. John J. English, *Spiritual Freedom: From an Experience of the Ignatian Exercises to the Art of Spiritual Guidance*, 2nd ed. (Chicago: Loyola Press, 1995).

us. The Hermitage of San Juan was beautifully positioned on a ridge overlooking the village of Oteo immediately below. The inside was simple and charming, with stone walls and rough timber, but water had done a lot of damage to the roof. José Maria proudly showed us the statues of St. Christopher, St. Francis, and St. John. In pride of place was a statue of the Virgin and child. We thanked him for the tour and started our way downhill to the village a short distance away.

Entering the village square, I said goodbye to the other two and arranged to meet them that night. Judiciously, I sat myself at the fountain in this rural village. The relief I felt from being still, was immediate and immense. *What to do now?* I thought. Walking was almost impossible for me, but it was unlikely there was a bus service here. The only option was to trust in providence. I felt the familiar thrill of placing myself in God's hands.[43] I watched the people passing for a sign or indication of where God might be at work around me. A woman emerged from a house with car keys in her hand and walked past. Seeing her open the car door, I thought I might ask her for a ride. But when she began to chat at length with her neighbors, I let it go.

Time dragged on, and I snacked on some nuts and fruit. I started to feel dejected and hopeless, but then a white van pulled in, blowing its horn repeatedly to attract customers. It was a daily delivery truck from a *panadería* (bakery). Many people appeared to pick up their daily bread. The address on the side of the van was the exact place where I needed to go: Santa Cruz. *This is it!* I sprang into action. I was out of luck—the driver said he was unable to help me because he had to make deliveries up into the valley. However, a bystander,

---

43. The pilgrimage experience in the Jesuit novitiate means that without money you are totally dependent on God; the key is to "hand everything over" and believe that providence is at work. Brendan McManus, SJ, "Ignatian Pilgrimage: The Inner Journey—Loyola to Manresa on Foot," *The Way* 49, no. 3 (July 2010): 95–108.

María, who overheard this exchange, asked me to wait as she went off to borrow a car. Another woman then offered to let me use her bathroom and led me down to her house, which was close by. It was quite overwhelming and heartwarming to be supported as a stranger in a time of need by the community.

A few minutes later María was driving me down the broad valley. I marveled at how effortlessly and painlessly we glided along. I was quiet, feeling extremely grateful for this miracle of goodwill and technology that was saving me so many painful steps. As we progressed down the valley, I spied a hunting bird with a great wingspan above us, and she told me it was probably an eagle or a hawk. These majestic raptors are often so close to us, soaring above busy highways and traffic. We are frequently oblivious to their presence, desensitized by urban environments and separated by our screens. We then came across a huge herd of maybe 500 sheep that were coming toward us. The shepherd with his staff strode at the front, and the rest of the sheep followed in a compact group, grazing on the hoof. I commented that it was a striking formation, how organized they were. María said the shepherd held them all together because he knows his sheep, and they know him. It was like John's Gospel on the intimate, organic relationship between sheep and shepherd. In that moment I understood why the shepherds in Urbia lived in those mountain huts I had seen a few days earlier. They stayed close to their sheep. They needed each other, a mutually beneficial relationship.

María dropped me right outside the Santa Cruz medical center. I was tired, hungry, and in pain, so I went to the main square to rest, eat another snack, and drink some water. Not really thinking straight, I decided to postpone the doctor and instead secure accommodation and get to Sunday Mass.[44] A passerby helped me find the nearby church, uphill a few streets away. As I circled the church looking for the door, I met an older man. He told me Mass would start in an hour and there was a *casa rural,* or rural guesthouse, only two streets away—my immediate needs were met (though I had avoided the medical exam!). I made my way down the steep cobblestones to the *casa rural,* but no luck: it was closed for the summer and the owners were on holiday.

Back in the busy main plaza, a younger couple told me there was another *casa rural* on a hill called Ibernalo, a little more than a mile out of town. They also told me to be sure to ring ahead. I thought on my rule of thumb: don't book ahead in order to follow the spirit of a true pilgrim. I needed a room, though, and I also knew I was unable to walk all the way there. I had to act against a growing desolation and immobility; it was crazy not to book just on principle (if there ever was a time for an exception). "*I can't be too rule bound*," I thought, and rang ahead to book a room.[45]

My business done, I made my way back to the church, Nuestra Señora de la Asunción, or Our Lady of the Assumption. Leaving my backpack and poles in an alcove at the side of the church, I presented myself in the sacristy to concelebrate as is customary for a visiting priest on pilgrimage. The priest, Fr. Antonio, gave me a great welcome and explained he was not the parish priest but was only helping out for this Mass. A theology lecturer in a nearby city, he had studied in Rome, and we knew some Jesuits in common. We were so busy chatting that we didn't notice that the time to begin Mass was on top of us. Processing to the altar, I realized that I would have to genuflect before the tabernacle, but I was unable to bend my knee! I hoped he would understand when I explained my situation to him afterward.

---

44. Ignoring my own guideline about trusting in providence is evident here due to negative feelings and tiredness; it points to some desolation and disordered attachment, not tackling the underlying medical issue (SE 1, 23, 63).

45. Rules and structures can be helpful up to a point, but the real sign of flexibility and interior freedom is the ability to adapt and shape them according to what the situation calls for, that is, discernment (SE 149–55).

He presented me warmly to the congregation and mentioned that they were happy to be receiving more pilgrims here because of the newly opened Ignatian Camino. He had asked me to read the prayers for intercession, and I rehearsed the Spanish prayers as he preached. Conversational Spanish was normally easy for me, but ritual prayers in a liturgical setting were nerve-wracking. Concentrating on getting the pronunciation right and protecting people from my Northern Irish accent was impossible. I had to go with it, hoping the congregants would understand.

After Mass, Fr. Antonio showed me around the magnificent church, which reflected many architectural styles, and we talked again at length. I was happy to accept his offer of a lift out to the *casa rural*—better than having to walk there! My friends Xavier and Iñigo were in the plaza as we walked to the car. I explained where I was staying and invited them to join me. They had decided to go on to the next town, though, so we said our goodbyes. It was unlikely we would meet again. This was the familiar Camino invitation to let people and things go.

The *casa rural* sounded ideal from what Fr. Antonio described in the car. It even had a hermitage right next door that I would love to explore. The *casa rural* was dramatically positioned on a wooded ridge named Álava, meaning "set among the mountains," with a view into a wide valley framed by cliffs all around. It was breathtaking—and a reminder of how many mountains were still ahead of me. Entering the bar, loud music, a track called "Noraezean," by a local band called Hesian was blaring. Suddenly feeling old and tired, I noticed knots of young people clustered around the bar. Eventually managing to attract the attention of the busy bartender, I registered for my room, and a young man showed me the way there. He listened with interest as I explained to him my pilgrimage and the Ignatian Camino. The room was small, shuttered, and lacked ventilation, and the blankets were cheap sleeping bags. Even though the location was beautiful, the room's view was blocked by trees out the back. It was luxury for a sore pilgrim, though, and I was set on making the best of things.[46] Food, shelter, and company—this was a huge bonus that I was very grateful for, especially given my plight just a few hours earlier. Back in the bar, I ordered lunch, and the same young man, Asier, was my waiter. We talked for a while about his job and his hopes for the future.

Escaping from the music, I sat out on the terrace in the afternoon sun. Soaking in the magnificent view—forest, cliff, field, and sky—and listening intently to birdcalls, I felt like the luckiest man alive. Reflecting on how hard it was for me earlier to go it alone on the trail, in pain, I recognized the dramatic change that came from resting and asking for help. Certainly, there was some pride in me, some competitiveness, and an unwillingness to own my weakness or face reality. Being literally brought to my knees was my catalyst for change, much as it was for St. Ignatius.[47] Determined to learn from all of my experiences and reflections on the Ignatian Camino, I committed myself to reflection and making necessary changes in my life. Real wisdom is knowing when to ask for help, not toughing it out. *What other help do I need to ask for?*, I asked myself.

It was a long and difficult evening. There was a heaviness in me that I couldn't account for. I passed the time watching TV, where the latest news featured the refugee crisis at the port in Calais, France. It was very distressing to see the desperation of the refugees, clearly visible in their faces, and also the efforts to accommodate them that didn't get at addressing the root of the problem. I went back out on

---

46. The practice of seeing everything as a gift opens my heart and transforms interactions and relationships. It is seeing as God sees (SE 233).

47. Ignatius's conversion was directly linked to the traumatic effects of the cannonball and his bodily wounds, which caused physical immobility and dependence on others, opening up new possibilities. W. W. Meissner, *Ignatius of Loyola: The Psychology of a Saint* (New Haven, CT: Yale University Press, 1992), 366.

the patio and had a drink. I found myself praying, through the inter-cession of the Virgin, asking for light, and handing everything about this walk over to her.

Conscious of the day's events, the idea of giving up on this Camino attempt popped into my mind. It was hard to consider because I was so invested in it. I had become trapped by my own expectations, ones based on my previous experience. I was finding it hard to let go of them.[48] I prayed for balance and for clarity about what God wanted for me.[49] I saw my two options starkly: quit and go home, or find some way to keep going. As I wrestled with the pull to quit or go on, I realized there was a third option that I hadn't con-sidered. I could continue the pilgrimage, not on foot but by public transport. This would be a great compromise: I could continue to the end and also solve my problem of not being able to walk so much. *Even if I arrive in Manresa, my final destination, by train, it will still be worth the journey*, I told myself. The relief was instantaneous.

The evening sun illuminated the contours of the valley, flush with pastel colors. Someone called my name from the terrace. It was Xavier. Iñigo had gone on ahead, and Xavier found himself in the next village with no accommodation. It was a joyful reunion, and we caught up on each other's day. I felt a spiritual connection to Xavier, and I felt free to share spiritual thoughts with him.

Xavier was born in Bilbao into a family with two sisters. He had a happy childhood, but as an adolescent, he lost his father to a heart attack. Some years later, his life was irrevocably changed when he witnessed a man

---

48. Ignatius defines freedom as "freedom for" living life fully and "freedom from" unhealthy attachments, such as compulsions or addictions. Freedom is not doing whatever I want but rather examining my motivations to see where I am caught and trying to move more toward what God wants (release from attachments) (SE 21).

49. Being balanced is about getting freedom from compulsions or negative attachments and being able to act consciously without being under their influence (SE 15, 179).

die in an accident; Xavier was powerless to help. It was then that he begin walking the Camino de Santiago, attending therapy and eventually church, looking for an answer to his questions. Some years later, he found himself at home with the prayer method of his fellow Basque, St. Ignatius. He happily applied himself to daily meditation and reflection. He calls this training the "school of the heart," because he learned how to listen with his heart to God's enabling love. Xavier told me that he still sometimes suffers from negative thoughts and feelings about the past. In those moments, he uses Ignatian awareness to concentrate on breathing, entrusting his thoughts to the Lord, and waiting patiently for inner peace to return. He told me that he had been working on a way to go through difficult moments in company. He finds consolation especially in singing with a choir, walking in nature with friends, and being able to express himself in his weekly Ignatian prayer group. Faith for him is knowing that when he wakes in the night with doubts or negative thoughts, he can persevere through the darkness to the light of morning, when he knows that peace will return.

Xavier and I chatted for a bit in the restaurant and then on the patio, which had a view of the valley—nearly invisible in the dark night—sprinkled with only a few lights. The conversation got serious as he shared with me an experience of loss and tragedy he had had some years earlier. Xavier was a searcher like me, trying to find peace with the past on his many walks on the Camino de Santiago and now the Ignatian Camino. He told me about an Ignatian prayer group that he was part of and mentioned several Jesuits he knew. We talked about Taizé again, our common experience of its peace and its inspiration that lit a fire within us. I told him about my brother's death and about walking the Camino de Santiago in my search of healing. We forged a strong bond that night. Then it started to rain, and we were driven inside. The warmth between us remained, and we agreed to meet the next day. Even though I wouldn't be able to walk with Xavier on the trail, I wasn't concerned anymore with keeping up. I was happy with whatever a new day would bring.

7

THE DOCTOR'S ADVICE

Despite such an enjoyable evening with Xavier, I hardly slept a wink. I was tossing and turning all night, trying to get into a position where my knee was comfortable. It did not work. Ragged and torn after the long night, I awoke entertaining the idea of quitting again. I thought of having to go home injured—and especially of failure. The night had magnified my fears and accentuated the worst of my situation. The thought that I might have seriously damaged my leg reinforced my thoughts that my trip was doomed. *I didn't handle the injury well and made it worse by walking on it. I should have taken more days to rest in Arantzazu. I pushed myself too hard—to the point of no return. I have no options but to quit now—I am so stupid!* [50]

As a gaping black hole of despair opened up before me, even as I tumbled into it I knew I had been here before. This was desolation, the decrease in faith, hope, and love. It was driving me further away from God.[51] I was falsely interpreting reality. To dig myself out of

---

50. The power of negative thinking can be arrested at its source; one needs to examine the whole sequence of thoughts to see where the change of mood happens. This means rooting out unhelpful or false ideas (e.g., I am useless) that are clearly not from God (SE 333–34).

51. In times of desolation, people are led by the evil one, who tries to bring people away from God. They are tempted to abandon a positive outlook and adopt deceptive thoughts as their own. There is an unease, a falseness, and a hollow ring that characterize it (SE 318).

desolation, I needed to reject all this negativity. *There is always a way out*, I thought. *I have options.* I took some time to pray for assistance. Gradually, it became obvious to me: I would go see the doctor at the town's medical center. My mood shifted.

Breakfast in the *casa rural* was a simple affair. Between mouthfuls, I told Xavier of my plan to go into Santa Cruz and see the doctor. I was ready to accept whatever medical advice the doctor would give me, and with that, freedom and lightness enthused my thoughts and spirits. I outlined my options with Xavier as we crunched along the gravel road into town, and he agreed with my plans. We embraced warmly as our paths separated at the outskirts of town. We didn't know whether we would meet again. We had found an echo of our experience within each other and had shared much on the journey. I was sad to see him go.

Walking through an awakening town on the way to the medical center, I braced myself for the possibility that this might not go as I wanted. Toying with the idea to conceal the extent of the pain, I realized this was the way of deception and deceit. It was spiritual desolation operating, and I would need to act against this by honestly telling everything as it was and accepting the doctor's diagnosis as final.[52] If he told me to rest, go home or to a hospital, I would be obedient to the doctor as the legitimate authority on these matters. As a Jesuit, I was accustomed to reporting to a religious superior, or "manager," and being transparent with the goal of allowing someone else, who could look at things more objectively, to help me make decisions. I needed to get free of my attachment to walking the Camino, as it seemed to be having a negative impact on my state of mind. I would let this doctor make the decision to go on or not for me.

---

52. Ignatius used this "acting against" (*agere contra* in Latin) as a key strategy for countering desolation, directing all your efforts to get back into consolation; counterintuitively, you often have to act against the way you feel and take decisive steps to get back on course (SE 13, 317, 322).

There was no queue at the clinic, and very shortly after filling in some forms, I was sitting in front of the doctor. His creased face and corduroys diffused any nerves I had, as did his warm and understanding manner. Explaining the situation was easy, except for a few Spanish words I lacked, like *limp* and *pain*. He examined my right knee closely, flexing, rotating, and pressing it every which way to identify the source of the pain. As usual when at the doctor's, the pain seemed to magically disappear, and I was frustrated that my words failed to convey the full extent of the problem.

The diagnosis was quite straightforward: "There is a sac of fluid on the kneecap caused by the impact when you fell. There is no real damage, though I would recommend a rest day and anti-inflammatories." I was relieved to hear this, a clean bill of health. But just to be sure, I outlined my plan for him: take the day off, skip eighteen miles of this part of the walk, and take up the Camino again in Laguardia, where the trail became much easier. A sense of gratitude and providence pervaded me. I had left my worries and anxieties behind in the face of what I considered an expert opinion. It was a classic Camino moment: I faced my fears and looked for help through an impossible situation.

At the council offices, I learned I would have to take a bus detour through Vitoria-Gasteiz, as there was no direct bus to Laguardia. *Fine with me*, I thought—just walking around the cobbled streets, soaking up the sunshine, was very fine indeed.

With three hours to wait, I made for the very attractive triangular town plaza, which had a stage at one end and was set into the hill. It was the natural confluence of roads and traffic and was full of life. I settled into a chair at a bar on the plaza, taking the chance to observe small-town Basque life. Pilgrims on the Camino don't just walk; they soak up local culture and have time to reflect on life. There was a quaint drinking fountain in the plaza flying a Basque flag. People sat around it, stood in nearby doorways, or sold their wares. I watched person after person come up and lean into it to drink the water. Even the baker came over from his shop to imbibe. I thought of how Christ is the fount of life (John 4:14: "Whoever drinks the water I give them will never thirst"), both for these villagers and for my fresh opportunity to walk again.

As I waited, a ragtag group surrounded the bus stop. There were young headphone-wearing students, neatly dressed workers, and slow-moving older people like me. On the bus, a young man greeted me warmly and invited me to sit with him. It was Asier; I remembered him from the *casa rural* bar the previous night. We took up the conversation where we had left off, sharing about our lives. I was happy to switch languages to help him practice his English. Neither the movement of the bus nor other passengers' chatter could shake us off our conversation. He told me that I was his favorite priest he had met and that he was once a believer but had seen too much injustice in the church. We took selfies together on the bus and hugged when we got off, not knowing whether we would see each other again.

Asier was twenty years old and from Bilbao; his parents were originally from Senegal. He worked in the casa rural *for two-week blocks to help him supplement his English studies in Bilbao. His girlfriend was going to London for an internship in medicine, and he was planning to visit her during Holy Week the following year.*

After my rural sojourn, I arrived in Vitoria-Gasteiz, capital of the Basque Autonomous Community, which is famous for its language, culture, and relative autonomy within Spain. It was like being in an alien world: neat and ordered, consumer focused, and all about image. A high-performance sports car passed me and a huge poster with a model promoting Dior perfume dominated a wall. The people looked bored and unhappy. It was a culture shock seen through my Camino eyes, where the focus had been on the inner journey and learning to be authentically human. I walked the streets around the bus station looking for a *menú del día* and eventually found a restaurant back in the bus station where I ordered lunch. On the music system was the group Boney M's disco version of "By the Rivers of Babylon," which was delightfully incongruous. The lyrics, based on the Old Testament Psalms 19 and 137, would work perfectly as a Jesuit prayer: "Let the words of our mouth and the meditations of our heart be acceptable in thy sight here tonight." At the same time, a plasma screen showed a reality TV show called *Cambio de look*, on which friends changed someone's appearance and clothes. Through my Camino eyes, it was superficial and pointless. I wanted to see inner change, transformational solitude, and a rejection of giving importance to outer appearances. I was regretting coming back to "civilization."

But then as I waited for the bus that would take me to Laguardia, a one-hour trip, I saw a woman saying goodbye to a boy at the bus stop. She wouldn't let him go. It was the most emotional of farewells; there must've been dozens of kisses dished out. There was nothing superficial about this emotion. Movingly, another younger woman led an older woman, maybe her mother, by the hand to get her to her bus on time. I was reminded that not all of society was tuned into superficial and materialistic values. Then it was time for me to get on my bus.

The journey was uneventful until we reached a steep incline, crested out on a ridge, then plunged down a steep hillside. The hairpin bends afforded great views of the limestone bluffs immediately above us and a massive plain below. This was wine country we were entering; this was Rioja. Vineyards cropped up everywhere, each with a grand entrance, offering wine tasting in their bodegas. I could see Laguardia from a distance, a fortified hilltop village that stood above the flatlands. The bus strained up the last hill and deposited me at the ancient walls. Tourists were already swarming, and I was in danger of getting knocked over as I limped around the main thoroughfare. I asked for directions to the tourist office, but most of the people there weren't locals. Eventually, I found it down one of the quaint medieval streets. A Belgian hiker was in front of me asking for information about walking the Ignatian Camino in reverse to Loyola, and I was glad to help and fill him in on accommodation and signage.[53] He was asking, as I was, about the cheapest accommodation in Laguardia, and we were both directed to the same place. There was only one option in this very touristy, expensive town, a guesthouse on the edge of the hill. I texted Xavier, whom I knew was still on the road, that we could share a room to reduce costs.

I made it just in time to Mass in the historic church of Santa María de los Reyes. Dating to the twelfth century, the church's tower has a Gothic façade and a striking polychrome portal. I rushed into the sacristy, and the priest, thinking I was a tourist, was a bit taken aback. I explained to him that I was a priest, and he was happy for me to concelebrate the Mass. In fact, he generously asked me to lead the Mass, but I declined because my Spanish wasn't up to that task. I did offer to read the Gospel, though, and prepared for that. Because of renovations, the Mass took place in the stunning portico of the main church. The church was packed because there was a novena, a Catholic devotion comprising Mass and special prayers over nine days, dedicated to the Virgin Mary. A motherly sculpture of her in the church dominated the figures of prophets, martyrs, and apostles.

As I was reading the Gospel and focusing on pronouncing the words well, I noticed the phrase addressed to Mary, "En cuanto a ti, una espada te atravesará el corazón" ("And a sword will pierce your own soul too," Luke 2:35). I don't know whether it was the striking church, the pain I had been dealing with over the previous few

---

53. Some Camino de Santiago pilgrims use the Ignatian Camino from Manresa to connect with the main routes westward to Santiago.

days, or tiredness, but those words touched my heart. I realized something of what Mary had suffered for her son because of the love in her heart. This was the same theme of love I had heard in Ignatius's devotion, that I had witnessed in the shrine of Arantzazu. *There's something important here for me*, I thought.[54]

Mary the mother of Jesus was likely born in Nazareth, a small town in Galilee that was looked down on by most Jews as a backwater. Mary, a Jew, would have spoken Aramaic and also known some Greek and Hebrew from the Torah recited in the synagogue. She was born into poverty, and her family got by through subsistence farming and small businesses or crafts. Their life would have been hard, burdened with heavy taxation and under the thumb of the ruling class. She probably lived with her extended family in a compound and spent most of her day in manual labor: helping cook, wash clothes, and carry water.

Mary was very young, probably thirteen or fourteen, when she was betrothed to Joseph, a much older man (this was common practice at the time). As a Roman census required them to return to Bethlehem, the teenage Mary gave birth to Jesus there. Far from our romantic image of a Christmas crib, Mary gave birth in an animal stable or pen, where conditions were very basic and not ideal. Rather than a fragile, brittle porcelain figure, this was a tough teenager capable of walking to visit her cousin while still pregnant, of making the yearly pilgrimage on foot to Jerusalem and carrying out onerous daily chores at home. Often portrayed

---

54. Devotion to Mary played a key role in the life and vocation of Ignatius, culminating in his conversion. Tom Casey, SJ, "Mary—how she made a new man of Ignatius," www.jesuit.ie/blog/tom-casey-sj/may-mary-made-new-man-ignatius/.

as fair and blue eyed, she likely would have had Semitic features and a dark complexion.

The early death of Mary's husband, Joseph, must have been a real blow. He seems to have died before Jesus' public ministry began. Mary herself lived through the time of Jesus' ministry alone, which must also have been painful for her. His brushes with authority and at times virulent opposition must have cost her. This would have been nothing compared to witnessing the crucifixion and death of her son as an elderly woman. Tradition has it that the risen Jesus appeared to Mary first, and she subsequently was one of the key figures in the early church. We are left with the lovely image of Pentecost, when the Spirit descends on Mary and the disciples. Mary is often known as Our Lady of Sorrows, referring to the depth of her trials and her heart full of compassion.[55]

Back at the guesthouse, I met up with a very tired Xavier, and we laid out our gear in the small twin room as best we could before heading out for food. Even the *menú del día* was expensive in this town, and we had to search to find a reasonable place to eat. Beautiful as it was, Laguardia was catering to more well-off tourists, not hikers and pilgrims on a budget. But sitting out on a restaurant patio, in the cool of evening, it was very good to catch up on how our day had been and all the providential things that had happened. It was a perfect "debrief," a processing of the varied experiences, and satisfying end to the day.[56]

---

55. Based on Robert P. Maloney, "The Historical Mary," *America*, December 2005, www.americamagazine.org/issue/555/article/historical-mary.

56. This is like a collective Examen prayer where a group can come together to reflect on their day. Simon Bishop, SJ, "A Collective Examen," www.pathwaystogod.org/my-prayer-life/examen/collective-examen2018.

8
RIOJA, UTOPIA

The payoff for the expensive aerie was a spectacular morning sunrise with mist descending from nearby hills and morning light illuminating the fortifications of the old city. The golden light in the room alerted me to a new day. An early riser, I was packed and out the door without waking Xavier. We had agreed to walk alone and meet in the evening.

The initial route was difficult and needlessly complicated, and I had to stop several times for directions. It was exhilarating to get back on the road again. Everything was looking up. With the mountains behind me and my injury sorted, I was looking forward to at least ten more good days of walking. Fired with enthusiasm, I thought, *Could I finish the whole trail?* The way I felt, anything seemed possible. I was wary of this new idea, however.[57] It felt good to walk unfettered among rows of vines and expansive vineyards, stretching as far as the eye could see. With the dramatic backdrop of the Cantabrian Mountains behind me, it was a flat plain in front. I had a close-up view of dusky grapes; I felt doubly blessed. I figured that most Rioja tourists wouldn't get a chance to see the vineyards so intimately. I watched a

---

57. Feelings of elation and euphoria often don't make for good decisions because of the temporary sway of powerful emotions. Ignatius would advise coming to a point of balance or calm before deciding (SE 15, 23, 179).

tractor plow around the edges of a field, preparing the ground for new vines, and a memory popped into my head of an old hurt done to me by a friend. *I have to let go of this too*, I thought, putting it to rest and allowing myself to be renewed. I pushed a stone into the loamy soil, a ritual for release and healing.[58] Then the next hour was a delight, passing vines loaded with grapes, alive to the morning sun, and enjoying easy walking—a Riojan utopia.

Arriving at the town of Lapuebla de Labarca, I made straight for the sixteenth-century church, Nuestra Señora de la Asunción, or Our Lady of the Assumption, where Mass was in full swing. I was a little late, but I figured God would understand the pilgrim's unpredictability and hunger for the Eucharist. Afterward, I introduced myself to the local priest, and he was very welcoming, telling me about a friend of his, an Irish priest who worked in the neighboring parish. Xavier had caught up with me at this stage for the end of Mass, and the priest invited both of us to the parochial house to get an official pilgrim stamp. He told us of an important visit that afternoon to the Sisters of St. Teresa of Ávila who were celebrating their 500-year anniversary. Outside, we met some parishioners who introduced themselves.

Xavier and I found a bar afterward for some much-needed food and drink. Out of the mountains, the heat was already above 70 degrees. As we waited for the order, the bartender was struggling with the espresso machine for our coffee—plugging and unplugging it, lifting it up, and finally banging on it in frustration. It was only at the end of this process that he thought to ring for help. Conscious of the importance of my medical consultation the day before, I wondered why we humans have to let things get so bad before we ask for help,

---

58. Handing over a painful memory to Christ means using the imagination to dialogue with the past and recognising our need for Christ's healing power. Jim Deeds and Brendan McManus, SJ, *Finding God in the Mess* (Chicago: Loyola Press, 2020).

struggling along with things not quite working and just making do.[59] Given this observation, it seemed to be a tall order for other people, too, not just me.

La Rioja is located in the wide, alluvial Ebro valley. Sheltered by the Cantabrian Mountains, it is warm and fertile, protected from the open plains to the south and the hilly Basque Country to the north. The grape vines thrive in the clay- and iron-rich soils of the valley. The result is a green and brown landscape in which everything is geared toward nurturing vines and their succulent grapes. Row after orderly row of vines swung into view in a sculpted landscape. I detoured into the vines several times to convince myself of the existence of the grapes, which were not visible from a distance. The dull sound of generators pumping confirmed that the nearby river was the source of all this fertility. Upon investigating, I realized that there was an invisible network of water pipes that was making all this possible. It is not what is on the surface that counts, but rather that which is hidden. I would think of La Rioja differently now. The Gospel story of the vine and the branches took on new life now that I had this concrete image of grapes nurtured through hidden water sources.

In the rapidly rising heat, I arrived in Fuenmayor and found its charming ancient streets empty, the town seemingly deserted. A woman carrying her shopping told me to go to the main plaza, find the mayor's office, and tell them that Sandra sent me. I accepted this clear invitation though I was tired and hot and I just wanted to collapse in the shade. I was happy to see the plaza packed with shops, families, bars, all sorts of social activities, and, most importantly, shade. Kids played tag through the mottled light between trees.

---

59. Taking the concrete steps to put one's life back in order, resisting procrastination and avoidance, is a cornerstone of the *Exercises* (SE 63). It is also essential to the 12 Steps of Alcoholics Anonymous. Jim Harbaugh, SJ, *A 12-Step Approach to the Spiritual Exercises of St. Ignatius* (Lanham, MD: Sheed & Ward, 1997).

I ordered a fizzy drink with ice; it was the most satisfying thing in the world right then. The mayor's office was not open, but I didn't care too much.

Leaving the shade, I had to trudge out of the village in the oppressive heat. It was even hotter out in the open, although mercifully a few clouds appeared, which would block the searing sun some. On the main road, I walked through a toll booth, free for pedestrians. However, there was no real footpath or provision for walkers, so I had to take to the roadway. Everything seemed designed exclusively for cars—it seemed this modern installation had thought little about pilgrims on the road.

As I walked the flyover from the toll booth, I could see the trail suddenly reappeared below to my right, but a steep incline and a chain-link fence prevented my passage. I could see where some people had climbed over the fence, but I knew with my knee that I wasn't capable of that sort of challenge. Doubling back, I found the underpass I had seen on the opposite side a few hundred yards back. I gingerly descended the steep concrete apron around it and took the underpass to the correct track.

The hill town of Navarrete, my destination for the night and a place Ignatius knew well, rose invitingly in front of me. A meeting point of the Camino de Santiago and the Ignatian Camino, I began to encounter waves of Santiago walkers coming from the East. Moved by the familiar sight of scallop-shelled backpacks, weathered faces, and telltale limps, I felt like I was meeting old friends. Shaking off my fatigue, I endeavored to greet everyone warmly. Local kids called out *buen camino*, or "have a good walk," as we all walked up the spiraling main street.

Hostels and bars abounded, cut-price rooms were advertised everywhere, and menus were in English for the first time on this walk. I was thinking I should soak my knee in a cold bath, but I was so tired that I simply went into the first place I came to. It was more expensive than I had planned, but two things dominated my thoughts: food and rest. After some stretches and the necessary washing of my hiking clothes, I crumpled into bed, rendered nearly a corpse. I felt happy and at peace, free of worries, but most of all, relatively free of this persistent knee pain. Gratitude permeated my being at having made it this far; even if I got no further, I had lived a great day. Who knew what would be granted to me tomorrow? I wondered if Ignatius had experienced these moments of total exhaustion, abandonment, and handing oneself over to God. I reflected that Ignatius always walked with a limp due to the damage done to his leg, and he was plagued by illness. However, the reappearance of the knee pain was troubling and vexing. Was I missing something here and "spiritualizing" some avoidable suffering?[60]

Coordinating by text, Xavier and I met for a cheap *menú del día* on the main street, but before we could order, the guy in charge, a German, told us there was a bullfight beginning in a few minutes. We let ourselves be swayed by the owner's enthusiasm. We joined the crowds going down to the town's bullring, a simple sand plaza with elevated seating. The spectacle was the carnival atmosphere, throngs of families, people young and old, all talking excitedly. A band played trumpets, flute, and drums to build up the atmosphere. Then out came a scrawny young bull, a *novillo*, a comic turn due to the ominous anticipation of a large threatening one. Lots of young men entered the arena to tease him, pull at him, and goad him with red cloaks. He raced around ever more disoriented; I felt sorry for the bull. Having seen enough, we left before things got too violent. On the way back, we passed a van with photos of *matadores*, bullfighters,

---

60. *Spiritualizing* means misinterpreting a physical or psychological issue (e.g., pain or suffering) as a spiritual movement (e.g., glorifying suffering uneccesarily), such that the resolution of the issue (e.g., medical advice and treatment) is hindered.

taunting huge bulls. *This must be what's next,* I thought. Escaping the crowd, I was glad I wasn't there to see it.[61]

In a sober mood, we chose to sit inside the cheap restaurant this time. We were mad with hunger. The meal was simple but good, and a glass of Rioja wine tasted like heaven. Preoccupied with satiating our hunger, we largely had a silent meal until our blood sugar began to rise. Then, over coffee, we returned to our conversation about life, faith, and meaning, as we had on previous evenings.

Xavier wanted to see the famous local church, María de la Asunción, but it wasn't open until later. I persuaded him to go with me on the Ignatian tour of the town. Ignatius had arrived here in 1522 with the Duke of Nájera to claim money owed him for his heroic service in defending Pamplona the previous year. Offered an important position, it must have been a real temptation to return to his previous lifestyle. He used the money to pay off some debts and to refurbish an image of Our Lady. In the Plaza del Arco, the former palace of the Duke of Nájera was marked by a badly worn stone shield, still visible in a corner. With the help of a local map and a fact sheet on Navarrete, we found the duke's former house that Ignatius had visited, formerly an inn where Ignatius had reputedly earned a bawdy pre-conversion reputation. Interestingly, Ignatius, on his way to Manresa, postconversion, stayed further down at Calle Arrabal No. 4, recently renovated as the Posada Ignatius guesthouse.

Eventually, we did manage to get into the magnificent church of María de la Asunción, which had an extraordinary altarpiece and a Baroque wall of statues, columns, and arches. I was preoccupied with finding the statue of the Virgin Mary that Ignatius had restored

61. This was a desolating experience where the crowd mentality overruled our own sense of discernment; only later did we reflect on what was happening and extract ourselves. It was a reminder that we are fallible instruments before God, needing to be constantly aware (SE 149–57).

with his wages in 1522. Finally, I found a young guide who was very knowledgeable about the church, and he assured me that it was the central one in the retablo, Virgen del Sagrario (Virgin of the Sanctuary). Spending some time with this statue, even under pressure from the sacristan to lock up, I felt I was very close to Ignatius. His devotion to the Virgin Mary was a theme that connected many places (Arantzazu, Navarrete, Montserrat). Certainly, his special devotion to Mary on the way to Montserrat helped protect him from falling back into his old habits and attachments.[62] The guide also took us into the sacristy, a trove of religious art, to show us a reliquary of St. Ignatius and an old picture that showed Ignatius writing his *Spiritual Exercises*. A thrilling end; as I walked slowly back to the hostel, I reflected that it had been a great day. And as a rock band was striking up in the main square, I was bound for bed.

---

62. Ignatius had a significant vision of Mary and Jesus while recuperating in Loyola that he attributed to his inner transformation from lust and vanity. He maintained this connection through the vow of chastity at Arantzazu and by carrying a Marian prayer book and an image of Our Lady of Sorrows.

9

AGAINST THE FLOW

I hardly slept, burning up with fever all night. *Surely it can't be my knee again*, I thought. Remembering the doctor's diagnosis, I discounted that right way. Pulling on my shorts and T-shirt, I joined some other hikers in the dining room for breakfast. Anxious to be on my way, I wound down the charming spiral road through the town. I was setting off a bit later than I had planned, but it was exquisite to be mobile, free of pain and on the road again. *What a story this will be!* I thought. I had struggled to work through injury and misfortune, and now I was consoled by this exciting idea of completing as much of the Ignatian Camino as I could!

The sun was well up when I reached the junction outside town where the Ignatian Camino and the French Camino de Santiago overlap. Santiago pilgrims were already streaming toward me as I went in the opposite direction. A hiker, his face glowing, stopped to check if I was going to Santiago, gently pointing out that I was going the wrong way. "I'm going home," I told him. I—to my Jesuit home, a permanent pilgrim on the road, "alone and on foot," just like St. Ignatius. Not for the first time in my life was I going against the flow. Whether leaving behind my previous job in information technology, joining the Jesuits and living the vows, or even trying to be still in a hectic world—all this went against a cultural current running

in the opposite direction. I remembered the Jesuit spiritual principle of *agere contra*, or acting against anything that didn't come from
God.[63] I knew from experience the cost of mindlessly going along
with things without engaging my inner compass. Here, my path was
taking me against the flow of the Camino de Santiago, a symbol for
walking my own path on the Ignatian Camino. I decided to greet all
my fellow hikers that I met with a cheery *buen camino*!

I continued to meet and greet many hikers on the trail. The Ignatian Camino runs parallel to the main road, and in the chain-link
fence separating the two, hikers had attached simple crosses made of
wood. Whether it was to remember the dead or for hikers to mark
their passage, the hundreds of crosses formed a wall of wood, a striking memorial. Gradually, I lost interest in greeting hikers—there were
so many of them—and I realized that something else was bothering me.

Slowly, almost imperceptibly at first, the dreaded pain deep in my
knee reappeared. *This is not possible*, I thought. *I am not feeling this!* As
a distraction, I began to focus on the individuals coming toward me
on the trail. One walker had a speaker-enabled backpack, so I heard
him before I saw him, blasting the song "Take My Breath Away," by
Berlin, for everyone to hear. I tried desperately to ignore the pain
in my knee, but while descending a steep incline, the pain dramatically increased. The persistent thought that I was finished chased me
down. In front of me was the glistening reservoir lake of Grajera, and
beyond that, the city of Logroño beckoned only a few miles away. At
the head of the lake a number of ducks bobbed around on the choppy
water as storm clouds blew in.

---

63. This is the principle of acting against pressure, inertia, or negativity, anything that
will throw you off your path or close down life-giving possibilities. It is a radical
commitment to prioritizing Christ over everything else (SE 13).

Returning to a fierce focus on the trail, I passed two cyclists wearing color-coordinated gear and head cameras; they were serious people of some intent and purpose. Awhile later, I passed a couple on a tandem also wearing identical outfits. It seemed to be the day for coordination. *I wouldn't like to be the rider at the back*, I thought. As they passed I could see the rider's face contorted with effort and his head hanging off to one side to see ahead of the bike. I shifted to pay attention to the T-shirts of passersby: Love Is My Drug, Get Fit Don't Quit, Wi-Fi Password, Glorious, Stay Real, You Are the Prettiest When You Are Happy, Let's Do This, Amazing Choice (with palm trees), A Patriot Is Better Dead, and Get Off My Block. These were a welcome distraction from my pain.

A lakeside café with customers laughing and enjoying themselves did nothing to help my worsening mood. The thought *This is so unfair* rose angrily from within me. I had expected that my experience would be like the last time on the Camino de Santiago, when God had appeared at the eleventh hour and everything had been miraculously transformed. Where was God now? I had prepared well and had given myself to this walk as before, but the expected peace and consolation had not arrived. Anger and frustration dominated my spirits. Where was God in this mess? How could God have betrayed me and let me down so; I felt cheated and abandoned. I was done with this whole walking thing, with the Camino and, in anger, with God too for that matter. I thought about how I had given myself to helping the bereaved during the last two years; surely I deserved some consolation now?

I had to accept once and for all that there was no way this pain would stop anytime soon. Right then, I knew my walk was finished. I felt a crushing sense of defeat and failure. Every step I took was excruciating. I wanted to go home. *Where are you now, God?* I asked.

On the outskirts of Logroño, at a statue of two Camino hikers, I asked a stranger to take my photo, to mark the end of my Camino, even though I was sullen. Walking barely more than sixty miles, it was surely the shortest Ignatian Camino attempted. I would drag myself off home and say very little about this Ignatian debacle. *Such an ignominious end*, I reflected. I had imagined finishing the walk triumphantly, not as a dusty, sweaty mess of soreness and aches.

Threading my way through Logroño's narrow streets, I saw that many people were carrying bread, big, brown loaves that protruded from bags of all types. I was famished, and seeing all that bread fueled my urgent desire for food and lodging. I was within a block of the Jesuit community where I planned to stay, but I had to stop and sit down on a park bench to collect myself, not wanting to arrive irascible and tetchy, taking it out on whatever unfortunate answered the door. The pervasive smell of cigarette smoke in the outdoor air was irritating me. Two women seated next to me were trying to have a conversation while a child moaned and whined in its mother's arms. I couldn't rise to the occasion of savoring my last few pilgrim moments.[64] Part of me knew that I was failing to appreciate the gift of just being there, being alive.

Once inside the Jesuit community house, the welcome was spontaneous and genuine. The guestmaster brought me up in the elevator, found me a room (what luxury compared to the guesthouses I had been staying in), and set some food before me. In between mouthfuls, I explained my situation, my sore knee, and my resolve to fly home. One of the older priests, José Ignacio, kindly brought me to a pharmacy to buy a bandage for my knee and some analgesics. "I don't want you to worry about anything; stay here with us as long as you like,

---

64. Illness, hunger, and fatigue are basic human needs that overpower discernment or good decision making. Knowing oneself to be off center, out of balance, it's better to postpone decision making and resolve the basic issues first (SE 179).

free of charge," he told me. I was moved by his generosity and care for a stranger. His bright disposition was infectious.

In the pharmacy, José Ignacio knew the owner and shop assistants and greeted everyone warmly. The assistant showed him a photo on her mobile while she was in the middle of helping someone else. The woman beside us had a club foot and a pronounced limp. That put my problems into some much-needed perspective. On the way back, I noticed José Ignacio was limping too. "It's arthritis," he breezed. "I'm older than eighty," he said, shrugging it off. We spoke of St. Ignatius having a limp for most of his life and wearing it lightly. Arriving back at the community, I asked why Ignatius had changed his name from his original Basque name, *Íñigo*. José Ignacio told me Ignatius probably felt it would be a more useful translation of his name in France and Spain. He explained the name's Latin origin, the word *Ignis*, which means "fire." That struck me as appropriate, given the Jesuit use of the theme of "hearts on fire."[65]

> *José Ignacio, eighty-seven years old, was born in La Rioja, the sunny region full of vineyards, orchards, and wheat fields. His family and culture influenced his sunny disposition and positive outlook on life. Having once been director of various schools and programs, he compares his life in its autumn to a peaceful sunset. His greatest joys have come from life itself, as he sees himself as created by God and part of the variety of creation. He has endured moments of great darkness by keeping his eye on God the Creator and living the faith of the psalmist in Psalm 15:8: "For with him at my right hand, nothing can shake me." Many years ago, José Ignacio made a deal with his Creator: "You take care of me, and I will take care of you," and it is this that has carried him through difficult moments.*

---

65. This phrase is often used to capture the commitment to Christ and apostolic zeal that results from doing the Spiritual Exercises. It is based on the Scripture quotation from Luke 24:32 where the two men on the road to Emmaus reflect with Jesus and have their desolation transformed. Michael Harter, ed. *Hearts on Fire: Praying with Jesuits* (Chicago: Loyola Press, 2005).

His personal philosophy of life is to enjoy everything and everyone each day as much as possible, infecting others with his enthusiasm and joy and tolerating others' idiosyncrasies. He believes firmly in the Resurrection and the hope contained in the words of Jesus that all will be one in Christ (John 17:20–21). He believes in human freedom to choose—that in this imperfect world there are good and bad choices as a result of a gift we have been given. He looks forward to meeting God face-to-face, to give thanks for all and to embrace his creator Lord.

After a much-needed rest, in the afternoon I explored the school and the parish buildings, admiring a fine statue of the pilgrim Ignatius. In much better spirits after the food and companionship, I happily attended Mass in the parish. The Gospel reading was the laborers in the vineyard (Matthew 20:1–16), and I was struck by the laborers' grumbling about the latecomers getting paid as much as them. The laborers were angry because they had worked all day in the heat, and the latecomers had worked less time but were still paid the same. It was the sense of unfairness and complaining about God's generosity that spoke to me; I felt like I had worked hard "in the heat" these last years. Having expected great things for my walk on the Ignatian Camino and feeling like I got very little back, I had been living those very emotions on the trail. *How can I learn from this parable*, I thought, *with its specific message for me?*

After Mass and a glass of Bénédictine liqueur, I enjoyed a terrific night's sleep. I woke up refreshed and energized. The decision about what to do next loomed large, and I needed to focus on a good discernment process: trying to find out, through sifting through my inner movements, what God wanted of me and for me. My knee was unquestionably painful to walk on and the idea of continuing on the Camino to Manresa seemed like self-inflicted punishment. However, I was finding it hard to let it go. As had happened on my previous 2011 walk, I found it difficult to accept the "failure" of stopping the walk, and the challenge for me was accepting the reality of the situation as God's will, not my own.[66] I also was running low on money, and my options were limited. The remaining choices were as follows:

1. **Go straight home.** The most obvious option was to simply go home as I had planned the day before, cutting my losses and getting medical help there. However, this felt too impulsive. I knew my injury wasn't life threatening.

2. **Take the bus or train.** My original goal had been to visit the Ignatian sites along the route, not necessarily to walk the whole thing. Navarrete, where I had just been, was the last important site for some considerable distance. I could take the train to Barcelona and visit the important sites there. My heart thrilled at the thought of visiting Manresa and Montserrat.

3. **Continue walking.** Even though this was obviously a non-starter, I was struggling with whether I was giving up too easily on the Camino, whether my knee was really that bad (*Was I imagining things?*), and there was the obvious attraction of continuing to walk with Xavier, who had been a great companion.

I considered these various options in my heart for some while, giving myself over to one option or the other to see how I felt about each one.[67] There was certainly a jarring sense of unease when I thought about continuing to walk. Going home felt like the safe but dull option. Taking the train to Manresa had a certain "daring adventure"

---

66. In 2011 on the Camino de Santiago, I was faced with a similar decision, though back then it was as a result of time pressure in order to finish the walk. Here, it was as a result of growing pain and desolation that was forcing the decision; I needed to be much more proactive and decisive.

67. The imagination is used to "try on" different options to see how they fit without committing to them. We can project ourselves into different scenarios and glean a lot of information and feelings that can be useful in discerning or sifting options. Elizabeth Liebert, *The Way of Discernment: Spiritual Practices for Decision Making* (Louisville, KY: Westminster John Knox Press, 2008).

feel to it. Eventually, I came to peace: I would stop walking. I wouldn't go directly back home but would go on to Manresa as an injured pilgrim. As I was concerned that I might have done some permanent damage to my knee, it was a bit risky to continue, but with some care, it could be done without exacerbating the situation.

Accordingly, it was with mixed emotions that I contacted Xavier, who coincidentally was still in Logroño, to talk about my plan. We met for a final drink in the main plaza. I told him about my decision to skip ahead to Manresa. Xavier shared that he also was deciding whether to go home or continue walking, that it wasn't clear to him which path he would take. I explained how I thought discernment could help him, and also helped him make a list of pros and cons for each option to draw out his various motivations and priorities.[68] Xavier made four columns and listed the advantages and disadvantages of the decision to stay on the Camino or to go home. Then, I offered to play devil's advocate with his decision by challenging his reasoning and pointing out possible problems. This was just like being a spiritual director, where I try to help people gain objectivity by relating their personal thoughts to me (a trusted other) to get another perspective.

Xavier decided to return to Bilbao, but from there he would continue the Ignatian Camino's spiritual process as laid out in his guidebook.[69] This involved going through the daily steps of asking for a grace, reading Scripture, reflecting on his experience, and praying on his own. He planned to go for a one-hour walk every morning to help him in this process. I offered to contact the local Jesuits to see if they

---

68. In my case, it was clear cut that I would stop the walk, but Xavier needed to weigh the consequences. This more rational approach to deciding can be a good introduction to discernment, as it asks the person to consider different angles and begin to realize the different emotional influences (SE 181).

69. José Luis Iriberri and Chris Lowney, *Guia del Camino Ignaciano* (Bilbao: Mensajero, 2015), 173–218.

might know of a spiritual director to help him on his "pilgrimage." Xavier accepted.

This was our last conversation, and our impending leave-taking lent a certain poignancy to our exchange. We talked about how it was possible to find God's will, about how to make it part of our lives without it getting swamped by the busyness of life. He knew about ways of coming close to Jesus, asking for the grace of being a companion of Jesus, and having a conversation with God using his imagination.[70] Xavier related how difficult that was for him to actually do, and he questioned how he could speak to God as a friend. I shared with him that God continually uses all means to reach us but that the use of our imagination can be particularly helpful to become close to God because it is so intuitive, intimate, and personal. If we can imagine talking with one of our best friends, why not use that facility with God? Xavier shared with me that when he prayed, he listened to his breathing, tried to stop his thoughts and head from taking over, and sought calm. The next step for him would be to bring his whole self to God, to engage in a dialogue. This means engaging the emotions, even at the risk of getting mad at God, bringing the joys and despairs of our lives into the conversation, trying to get some help and insight, and finally taking concrete action.

I told Xavier my own story about how I had transitioned from yuppie to Jesuit beginning with a Benedictine retreat twenty-six years earlier. Arriving on the Isle of Wight back then, I didn't really know how to pray, but I knew that I wanted an answer to the desolating and unfulfilled life I was living. This was only the start of a two-year process, step by step toward my goal, much like the Camino. I felt that God had been calling me for a good while, disturbing my false sense of peace, stirring up my emotions, planting people

---

70. Known as the colloquy, in the *Spiritual Exercises* Ignatius encourages the person to talk with Jesus as "one friend talks to another" (SE 54).

and life-changing challenges in my path. Significantly, I told him, it was the discomfort, unease, and life-sapping desolation that forced me to pay attention to my inner life. Eventually, I got the message that the corporate lifestyle was not for me, that God was indicating another path. We got to talking about the discernment of spirits, how there are two sets of discernible forces working on us, which he already knew a bit about. I showed him the key passage in his copy of Ignatius's autobiography of the experience of the different spirits working on him during his recuperation and his subsequent reflection. He uncovered the workings of God in his life, the clear direction away from his past vanities, and a new life as a pilgrim in the service of a new Lord.

The Plaza del Mercado in Logroño was a busy place. Our conversation that day ranged over a variety of topics—sin, grace, forgiveness, and vocation. We had walked and talked together over many things and shared meals and miles on the trail. We parted with great emotion. I thanked Xavier for being such a wonderful companion; he thanked me for being his *asesor*, or adviser. It was a privilege to have the opportunity to help others as I had been helped.

Back in the Jesuit community that night, with a train ticket to Barcelona in my pocket, I was restless and uneasy. I felt alone and uncertain about what was next. Wandering around the rambling building, I found a ladder accessing a rooftop walkway. Using my phone's flashlight to light my way and withstanding considerable pain due to my knee, I climbed up. The stars were out, and as I lay down on the roof, still warm after a day's sun, I could see beyond the city lights into a vast night sky. I thought of Ignatius, the stargazer, who loved gazing into the night sky, looking to the heavens as a sign of God's presence. I understood his fascination in a new way. *Will this trip be a long experience of metaphorical death and rebirth?* I wondered, while supine on the surface of the world.

10

THE LONELY VIGIL

The fast train from Logroño to Barcelona hurtled through the Spanish countryside. I felt a certain ignominy as a pilgrim resorting to public transport, even though it was more than justified on this occasion. An intriguing scenery of fields, towns, and hills rocketed past in a disorienting blur. In the train car, I shivered slightly in the air conditioning, watching all the passengers slowly rock together in stony silence. I stretched out my knee past the backpack at my feet praying that my pilgrimage would take a turn for the better with this final journey to Manresa.

I ended up in Barcelona's Sants railway station, from which I took the subway directly to Plaça Espanya for the local train to Montserrat. The name *Montserrat* means "jagged mountain" or "saw-toothed mountain." This alone was enough to evoke images of a remote monastery surrounded by steep precipices and clouds. The Benedictine shrine to Our Lady of Montserrat, with its venerated statue of the Black Madonna and child, was where Ignatius realized some key aspects of his transformation. Handing over his sword during a dramatic all-night vigil at the altar of Our Lady, he committed himself to Christ, his new Lord. Then, dressed in sackcloth like a beggar, he cast off his old life.[71] When I stayed in the monastery as a Jesuit novice some twenty-one years previous, I wanted to understand this huge inner and outer transformation. Maybe my return as a pilgrim would give me fresh insight. Particularly, I had a great desire to replicate Ignatius's all-night vigil, to understand more of his own transformational experience.

On the train, the emerging profile of Montserrat's serrated peaks, a testament to time and geologic pressure, loomed ever larger. Rocks, gravel, sand, and clay deposited by rivers millions of years ago had been elevated by shifts in the earth's plates, then sculpted and shaped by erosion to form curiously rounded pillars and bands of gradated rock. It spoke of powerful pressures, hidden processes, and great transformations—what a site for a Benedictine monastery! As the local train arrived at the base of the cable car, the fast route up the mountain, I saw the signs for the parallel hiking path to the monastery, 1,600 feet straight up. A mad idea seized me that I could walk up. I imagined myself laboring among the crags and peaks, emerging victorious. Snapping out of the daydream, I couldn't believe I was even entertaining such a thought. There was apparently a certain seductive temptation, or fault line, in me that prioritized determination and dubious achievement.[72] In the end, I managed to regain some balance and peace and decided firmly to take the cable car. Reassured, I was happy to experience the view, and I acknowledged that this same misdirected idealism had often misled me before.

The silent cable car whisked me up into the heart of the Montserrat peaks. The sheer verticality of the cliffs right beside the monastery emphasized the precariousness of the dwellings that were wedged in

---

71. Ignatius is the only saint known to have dedicated himself through a vigil of arms, a throwback to chivalry and romance, as a ritual of change of life and new allegiance. James Brodrick, *Saint Ignatius Loyola: The Pilgrim Years, 1491–1538* (San Francisco: Ignatius Press, 1998), 79–81.

72. The most difficult temptation to discern is that which appears to be good on the surface but actually undermines health and well-being. In Ignatian language, the bad spirit is disguised as an angel of light to deceive the good person (SE 332).

narrow gullies. I couldn't help but notice further up a whole series of cables, steel nets, and reinforced sections that provided necessary protection against rock fall. Close up, the rock color was a reddish gray, a composite of clays, rocks, and marls that formed soft curves and domes. It was not difficult to see why the original Benedictine hermits would have chosen this location—its remoteness and ethereal beauty. Despite wars and reforms, the Benedictine monastery had become a world-renowned place of pilgrimage. Now, I was determined to see the spot where Ignatius held his vigil of arms in 1522 and the statue of the Black Madonna. Miraculously, I felt like a pilgrim again!

Benedict was born to a wealthy family in Norcia in Umbria, central Italy, in about 480. He attended school in Rome, and then, while still a young man, turned his back on the world. According to Pope Gregory, "giving over his books, and forsaking his father's house and wealth, with a mind only to serve God, he sought for some place where he might attain to the desire of his holy purpose."[73] Initially he lived in Enfide, seeking the company of other ascetics, in the Simbruini Mountains near Rome. There, Benedict met a monk, Romanus of Subiaco, whom he imitated in donning the monk's habit and living an extreme life as a cave dweller on the mountain. Local shepherds would mistake Benedict for a wild animal, such was his appearance. The story goes that these shepherds were converted as soon as they talked with Benedict.

His time as an anchorite, or solitary hermit, was short lived. Benedict's exemplary spiritual life of discipline and prayer earned him a reputation for holiness, and people came to seek his advice. Of particular interest was his vision of genuine monastic life. Over the following years, he constructed a number of monasteries. In

73. "Benedict of Nursia," New Word Encyclopedia, www.newworldencyclopedia.org.

each, he had a system of a governing superior with a small number of monks. During this time, a number of miracles were attributed to him. In the final years of his life, he drew up his famous Rule for governing monastic life, unique in its moderation and balanced approach. He died at Monte Cassino on March 21, 547, at the age of sixty-seven. The community of Montserrat, founded in the tenth century, is composed of a hundred monks who are governed according to this same Rule of Saint Benedict, devoting their lives to prayer, welcoming pilgrims and visitors, and performing various works.

Bells rang out like laughter in the clear air. I was in time for Vespers in the Gothic basilica, and it was at capacity. In the half light and with robed monks all around, and surrounded by a world of liturgy, incense, and chant, it was easy to feel like I was stepping back in time several centuries. It brought me back to other monasteries in England and Ireland where I had received great solace at tough moments of my life. There was something sacred about hearing traditional sung prayer, giving thanks for the day and offering praise to God as dusk approached. Despite all that had happened, I was so grateful just to be alive and to be witnessing the beauty of this moment of worship. I was especially aware of Black Madonna, out of sight in an alcove behind the main altar but present and alive in my consciousness. My reverie was punctured by the reading of Scripture: "Father, into your hands I commend my spirit" (Luke 23:46 quoting Psalm 31:5). The words, which came from the mouth of Jesus on the cross, are a psalm of hope in deliverance. The third verse from the same Psalm, "you are indeed my rock and my fortress," seemed to reverberate off the walls. It felt like a message specifically to me on this pilgrimage to let go and let God be in charge.

As I came out from the sanctuary onto the main plaza, the sun was setting over Catalonia. I sat down to have a drink in the view of cliffs and clouds. After registering with the pastoral office, I was invited into the monastery for supper. My minder, Fr. Benedict, met me at the door. Having spent a night there years before, I knew the routine and joyously watched the monks filing in. With around twelve other guests at the top table, we all ate in silence, listening to a reading in Catalan about Napoleon, who had destroyed the monastery in the nineteenth century. Over the years, the one thing I had learned about Benedictine meals was to eat quickly, before the food was removed!

Fr. Benedict had asked me to meet outside the four-star hotel, Abat Cisneros, after supper, and for a brief moment, I thought I might actually be staying there. From there, though, he led me further down the street to the youth hostel, which was a considerably humbler accommodation. I deposited my backpack on a bunk and accompanied the monk back to the basilica. I had explained my desire to do the overnight vigil with the Black Madonna, and he had made the necessary arrangements for me. I joined the monks for night prayer in the choir loft at the back of the basilica. I was transported to another time with the combination of sound, gesture, and ritual, which were all so elegantly woven into worship. The rendering of the Salve Regina was moving, beautifully sung and so simple. It brought me right back to Irish Jesuit funerals, where this is sung graveside. Thinking that one day it would be sung for me was comforting.

Ever since I first read the account of Ignatius holding the vigil of arms at the altar rails in Montserrat, I had dreamed that I would do the same. When I had been here as a novice, I wanted to divest myself of the trappings of my old corporate lifestyle and give myself completely to God.[74] There hadn't been time to do the vigil then, and I had always regretted the lost opportunity. This could be a watershed moment on this trip, I thought. All I have to do is give myself totally in this penitential vigil. This was my chance to live the experience of Ignatius fully, gain some insight into his transformation and the role of the Virgin in it. I was given a key so that I could get access after dark, and, thrilled, I made my way up to the ornate silver and gold chapel behind the famous statue of the Black Madonna. Located right in the heart of the sanctuary, this small chapel has an intimate stillness about it.

After the main lights had been turned out and the monks disappeared, I settled in for the long night. There was total silence. Anticipating this deep period of prayer, to be alone with God, and in the company of the Virgin, I closed my eyes. To my horror, within a short space of time, I had fallen asleep. I couldn't believe it. Frustrated, I shook myself and tried to stay awake. As Ignatius recommends, I tried kneeling and walking around the back of the chapel, but as soon as I sat down, I fell asleep again.[75] Wakened by the sound of a pipe organ being switched on, I looked down and saw a monk organist and two friends in the choir loft below winding up for a performance. They were clearly unaware there was a pilgrim at vigil in the chapel above. The organist began a long and complicated series of scales and chords that spiraled off into dark ecclesial echoes.

I doggedly resumed my attempt at inner silence, pressing into service everything I'd learned about distraction. Eyes closed, I fell off a cliff of unconsciousness and came to with a start, completely disoriented. It showed one am on my watch. I realized I was in no shape

---

74. This was the chivalric custom for knights entering into the service of a new lord, to maintain a vigil of arms the entire night. Ignatius divested himself of his fine clothes and wore a pilgrim's outfit, in his desire to pledge allegiance to his new Lord. George E. Ganss, ed., *Ignatius of Loyola: The Spiritual Exercises and Selected Works* (New York: Paulist Press, 1991), 26.

75. The use of the body and different postures, mirroring our inner disposition (pleading on your knees), can be helpful for focusing prayer (SE 76).

to do this vigil. The organ music, now György Ligeti's organ solo "Volumina," had taken on a more sinister and eerie tone that drove me hobbling down the vast corridors and out into the night.[76] My head was throbbing now, and my whole body was exhausted. I was spent and desperately craved sleep, an escape from pain. I was learning about accepting limits and recognizing clear signs.[77] Arriving at the student hostel, I fumbled for the key and rushed straight for my bunk. A blinding headache was pressing me down. Coming to around six in the morning, the three hours of sleep had been enough to restore my calm and sanity. Rooting through my backpack, I could hear the infernal music beginning to play again in my head. *Was it my imagination? Could I really hear the manic organ playing that cacophony of minor chords?*

I slipped back into the monastery and up the labyrinthine corridors to Our Lady's shrine as dawn was breaking. The Black Madonna regarded me serenely, as though she sensed my emotions of disappointment and failure. Bringing myself and all my baggage from these last few weeks to her, I still had a strong sense that Mary was on my side, lovingly presenting me to God. Ignatius, who had lost his own mother at an early age, would have understood this appeal through "the mother to the Father." I began a conversation with Mary, conscious of my obvious faults, and trusting in her compassionate heart.[78] Just as for Ignatius, Mary was easy to confide in and pointed the

---

76. Given the evocative power of music, I imagine that today Ignatius would have harnessed music as part of his Spiritual Exercises to relish and savor experience (SE 2).

77. This was an example of a "head" inspiration for doing the vigil, whereas it was clearly not a good idea as my body was telling me otherwise. Jemma Simmonds, "Making Sense of Application of the Senses," www.jesuit.org.uk/articles/ making-sense-application-senses.

78. Mary's role in the Exercises is always in relation to Jesus, and praying through her gives us access to the heart of Jesus in a powerful way, especially in the Passion (SE 298).

way to God. My own sense of consolation grew with the increasing daylight, and I looked around, marveling at my surroundings in the glittering chapel. I had gotten through the night thanks to the Madonna. The monk, who opened the shrine doors for the day's tourists, found me bolt upright, bright eyed, and bushy tailed. He left quickly, respecting my silence. *He thinks I have been here all night*, I thought wryly. *I'll have to come clean on this later to Fr. Benedict.* The monk kindly invited me down to the main chapel for morning prayer, and we processed down in silence. Prayer was an intoxicating experience of sung psalms, antiphons, and readings.

In contrast to the monastery, the guest dining room for breakfast was a riot of people and conversations. I sat beside Louisa, a Catalan woman from near Girona. She was part of a group of parish choir leaders learning Gregorian chant. Louisa told me about their weeklong course at the monastery and introduced me to a number of her peers as a Jesuit father *walking* the Ignatian Way. I clarified that I was by then actually traveling by public transport and told them about my knee.

In true Benedictine style, the main Mass that morning at eleven was a well-crafted liturgy of music, solemn movement, and symbols of worship. The Gospel reading and the paradox it contained caught my attention: "For all who exalt themselves will be humbled, and those who humble themselves will be exalted" (Luke 14:11). Again, I felt like those words were specifically meant for me. They spoke to me about the humility I had to have to accept my injury. The ignominy I felt for failing to keep the all-night vigil and for not having walked the entirety of my planned pilgrim route was undeniable. The Gospel spoke to my sense of failure and offered me a more hopeful interpretation of my current situation. This whole experience was teaching me humility, stripping away my pride and self-reliance, and forcing me to be more open to what God wanted for me. It seemed to me that, like the experience with the Madonna and with others whom I had met on this journey, these unexpected encounters were the real treasures. Being injured had in fact brought some surprising blessings.

After Mass, in the main plaza, it was peak tourist hour, and guides surged up the thoroughfares with the groups of tourists they were leading, cameras projecting like defensive spears. With a heavy heart, I knew it was time for me to leave Montserrat. Those precious moments of solitude in the Madonna chapel that morning came straight to mind. Seeing that iconic statue made me feel a little closer to understanding Ignatius. What stood out for me the most was identifying with Mary's great humility, her tremendous freedom in taking on the divine plan, and her commitment to her Son to the end. It seemed to me from my fitful vigil experience that, in Montserrat, Ignatius gradually moved more toward what God wanted rather than what great deeds he himself could accomplish: a shift from willfulness to openness. Here, Ignatius donned his pilgrim's attire, placing himself at the service of a new Lord, and began an itinerant life more aligned with the poor. The mountain refuge, a place of transformation, cemented his transition to a new pilgrim life dedicated to discerning the road ahead with God.

After thanking those who had assisted me, I took a virtually empty cable car to the base of the mountain. It was a bit disheartening coming down into the hot flatlands after those magical, mystical heights. I had perhaps expected something spectacular, an eleventh-hour healing in this special sacred place. A man on the platform helped me get the right train to Manresa, my next Ignatian destination. I mentally reviewed what I knew about that place. The cave came to mind, the organization of Ignatius's spiritual experiences into his conversion, dealing with scruples and fine-tuning his discernment or decision making—it sounded like exactly what I needed.

THE CAVE OF THE CONVERSION

On the train to Manresa, I had my choice of seats, and we arrived very rapidly. Manresa is a town dominated by the La Seu basilica, the Cardoner River bridge, and the Jesuit retreat house. Consulting the local map at the station, I balked at having to walk all the way through the old town to get to the Jesuit retreat house. I limped along, reluctant to put much pressure on my leg. The pavement was rough, and I made sure to watch my step, ignoring a lot of the medieval architecture. After some sharp descents and ascents, I reached the main door of my destination.

I rang the bell, but there was no answer at the door, except from an elderly man who told me to ring another extension. Eventually, a person on silent retreat reluctantly let me in and motioned for me to wait for the receptionist. I left my backpack by the front desk and went straight down to the cave, the place I had been looking forward to visiting. There are a variety of buildings on the site at Manresa: the Jesuit residence, the retreat house, and the Baroque church. The church is at the base of a cliff and is connected to the retreat house above it by an elevator. However, right beside the church is a natural grotto, or recess in the rock, that has a view to the Montserrat mountains. This cave is the iconic place where Ignatius prayed, experienced God, and formulated the *Spiritual Exercises*.

Stripped of a lot of the Baroque adornment, the walls of the cave had been brought back to a much simpler design. Although much of it was still covered in marble, some of the original rock was now exposed. The stone and honey light embraced me as I gratefully shuffled in to pray as a pilgrim. The gift of these three days was of having to let go of all my personal plans and hopes. I had a new desire to "see Jesus more clearly, love him more dearly, and follow him more nearly."[79] Chastened by my perceived failure on the Camino, I looked to know Christ more intimately, to be close to the Blessed Mother, and to ask for guidance and healing.

Having been unexpectedly wrapped up in prayer, I returned to find myself locked out of the retreat house and had to ask another person to let me in. Luckily, there was a room for me, and after gathering up my things, I headed upstairs. The room was the best I had been in yet, with an *en suite* bathroom and air conditioning—what a luxury! Exhausted but happy, I turned on the cool air, saying goodbye to the oppressive heat, and fell into a dreamless sleep.

In the morning, I had time to explore the extensive retreat house and residence. There were prayer rooms, chapels, balconies, meeting rooms, and lounges, all designed to facilitate reflection and meditation. All over the house were paintings, statues, and memorabilia associated with Ignatius and the Jesuits. Especially prominent was *Spiritual Exercises*, the retreat handbook Ignatius formulated based on his own experiences of faith and a key mystical experience here, at the river Cardoner. It was not difficult to imagine him in the cave wrestling with his scruples, struggling with his demons, and synthesizing his hard-won insights into guidelines for others.[80] Using my

---

79. The Exercises can be synthesised as a practical way of developing a close relationship with or interior knowledge of Christ (SE 104). Brian O'Leary, SJ, "Three Things I Pray . . .", www.catholicireland.net/three-things-i-pray/ (SE 104).

imagination, which is central to the Exercises, was useful in bringing Ignatius's experiences to life, especially in this place, the locus for many of them. Coming across a book of Ignatius's letters, I noted the key role of women in Manresa, especially Inés Pascual, who was a great supporter of Ignatius in Manresa as well as a subsequent witness in his beatification process.

Inés Pascual, a widow from Catalonia, first met Ignatius on the road from Montserrat in 1522 and was to become one of his biggest patrons during his time in Manresa and subsequently in Barcelona. Initially, she found him a bed in Santa Lucía hospital, as he was very weak and malnourished. She provided food and donations, even forgoing her own dinner for Ignatius: "She recalled that it consisted of chicken and a generous serving of broth which he really needed because he was so undernourished."[81] She maintained this support during the time he was in the hospital, although he continued to fast, prayed long hours, and was preoccupied with the poor.

Undoubtedly, Ignatius's holiness, humility, and desire for God made a deep impression on Inés, to the point that she committed her resources, influence, and energies to his emerging project. Until her death in 1548, Inés was his "sister in Christ our Lord," as described in letters Ignatius wrote to her. Inés, her son, Joan, and his family were witnesses to Ignatius's eight-day ecstatic experience at Santa Lucía.[82] Subsequently, she supported him in Paris

---

80. The Exercises are experiential in nature, based on the experience of Ignatius and inviting us to likewise experience God in concrete circumstances (SE 2).

81. Joan Segarra Pijuan, *Manresa and Saint Ignatius of Loyola*, 3rd ed. (Manresa: Ajuntament de Manresa, 1992), 51.

82. This chapel in the old Hospital of Saint Lucia was where Ignatius experienced an ecstatic spiritual rapture that kept him motionless for eight days. (ibid. 57–62).

with money for his living expenses and studies. Ignatius also wrote a letter to her to ask for financial support for himself and others. This and other letters give a sense of the deep gratitude Ignatius felt for Inés, the high esteem he held for her, and how intimately she was involved with this early "Jesuit" mission.

For Sunday Mass, there was nowhere more appropriate than the impressive Basilica Santa María de la Seu, standing proud over Manresa. Dating from the ninth century, the basilica is a monument to transformation through the times, wars, and styles, culminating in its Gothic design. Ignatius had an important mystical experience on the steps of this basilica, regularly received spiritual advice from the priests, attended daily Mass, and sang the Divine Office in the evenings there. My hopes for a serene High Mass were dashed when, upon entering, I saw a truck with drums and instruments being offloaded for a music festival outside. Soon enough, the liturgy and Gothic setting were punctuated by bursts of intense drumming from the street. It was a reminder of the interplay between church and world, lest they forget each other. Still, this church was a place of light and worship, and it was easy to imagine Ignatius being transfixed there.

In the afternoon, with the help of a guidebook, I did a self-guided Ignatian tour around Manresa. I felt like a detective piecing together Ignatius's movements. Fortunately, most of the places were near the retreat house and didn't involve much walking. It was a fascinating Ignatian "treasure hunt" to find places I had often heard mentioned: the Guia Chapel and Cross, where Ignatius first arrived in Manresa; the Hospital of Santa Lucía, where the saint experienced a spiritual rapture; the Pont Vell, a medieval bridge over the Cardoner River; the Well of the Hen, site of a miracle by the saint; and the Tort

Cross, where Ignatius had mystical revelations. I returned to the Pont Vell to finish my walk as it afforded a magnificent panorama of the main sites.

Back at the retreat house, I emailed Tony, the Jesuit who had been my novice companion in 1994 and was now working with the Jesuit Refugee Service. I told him about my disappointing "finale" this time. Tony and I had replicated Ignatius's pilgrim journey twenty-one years earlier, walking through hunger, fatigue, blisters, and insecurity. We had arrived joyously in Manresa. I even found the spot where we had taken our final triumphant photo with the jagged mountains of Montserrat in the background. *There isn't much triumph now*, I thought, the way things had worked out. *But maybe that is exactly the point*, as Tony helped me see. Being preoccupied with happy or dramatic endings—well, that isn't how life normally works out. Learning how to keep going through failure was an important skill. Besides, I had an inkling that there was something yet to unfold, if I could let go of some of the tyrannical expectations. The Gospel story of Jesus healing the Gerasene demoniac (Luke 8:26–39), tortured, living in the graves of the past, sprung to mind. The man was restored to his "right mind" through his contact with Jesus, returning to his normal health but not excessively changed.

By chance I met the organizer of the Ignatian Camino, José Luis Irriberri, SJ, and I filled him in on my eventful but "true to the Ignatian spirit" pilgrimage. An avid walker himself, he had been walking several days ahead of me on the trail. He brought me down to the church beside the cave and showed me the Jubilee Year Holy Door, which Pope Francis had inaugurated in 2015 for the special year of mercy and forgiveness internationally. This had been the original wooden door to the cave and marked the official end of the Ignatian pilgrimage. Despite my protestations about being an unsuccessful, wounded pilgrim, José Luis presented me with the official pilgrimage certificate and signed it for me. I was humbled by this recognition, especially since I technically hadn't completed all the requirements. As with my 2011 walk on the Camino de Santiago, I just barely qualified as I had taken all sorts of shortcuts. However, I knew this was more about the overwhelming nature of God's compassion than my personal efforts. It renewed my hope that God was not done with me yet.

At dinner, I met several Jesuits in the community and two others, whom I had met before, one of whom was from Sri Lanka and another from India. As the meal went on, I gained in Spanish fluency, and we had good fun teasing each other. José Luis mentioned to the others that I had written a book on the Camino de Santiago, *Redemption Road*. "The opposition!" exclaimed the older priest, and then said to me: "You will have to write one for us."

Laughing, I said, "I don't know if it would be the kind of book that will help promote your walk."

José Luis chipped in: "But if it had an angle on the Ignatian trail, a particular focus, like the wounded, limping Ignatius . . ." This helped me to put words on what had been forming in my mind these last days: another way of viewing this "fallen pilgrim" experience, from God's point of view, just as Ignatius had experienced in this very place. This was a helpful conversation and a great boost to be with other Jesuit companions. "Send me a copy" was the last thing José Luis said to me.

The next day, I decided to go to Barcelona, the last Ignatian site, where a close Jesuit friend, Enric, lived. I was coming to the end of this Spanish saga and running out of energy, ideas, and money. Before leaving Manresa, I made one last visit to the cave to reflect on the journey and gather my final thoughts. The carved image of Ignatius over the altar in the cave looked strange to me: his head is twisted back to look at the Virgin and child as inspiration for his writing the *Spiritual Exercises*. I read the account of his time in Manresa again.

It was an important place for Ignatius, originally just a detour that ended up in a stay of almost a year, where he was "taught like a child" about the things of God.[83] Here, Ignatius consolidated his new pilgrim lifestyle by fasting, begging, praying for hours, and letting his appearance go, effectively counteracting his previous vanity. In Manresa, the main learning would be about tempering excess and finding balance, though.

His initial spiritual peace was destroyed by scruples, an inability to let go of the sins of his past life, and the undertaking of severe fasts and penances. For the latter of these, his health would suffer for the rest of his life. Repeated visits to his confessor only resulted in greater levels of scrupulosity. Driven to extremes, Ignatius even contemplated taking his own life. His liberation was in realizing his dependence on his own efforts and in seeing that he was being misled by an "apparent good" (the focus on excess and effort). These temptations ended up damaging his health and taking away his peace. This realization about how he was being misled by his own thoughts was instantaneous and a great spiritual revelation.[84]

The insight Ignatius was granted became one of the key principles for decision making, or discernment, in his *Spiritual Exercises*. Although God is good, we also need to be conscious of negativity and the bad spirit lurking in our hearts. Just because something looks good doesn't mean it is; things can start off well but end up being harmful. In Ignatius's case, obsessive remorse over his previous life

---

83. Joseph N. Tylenda, *A Pilgrim's Journey: The Autobiography of Ignatius of Loyola.* (Collegeville, MN: Liturgical Press, 1991). No. 27.

84. He was misled by an apparent good, called the "angel of light" deception (SE 332): having remorse for sins was a good thing in itself, but taken to excess, scruples nearly killed him, tormenting him to the point that he thought to take his own life. Brian Grogan, SJ, *Alone and on Foot: Ignatius of Loyola* (Dublin: Veritas, 2008), 65.

became harmful when he took it to the extreme. Ignatius was to subsequently regret the damage done through harsh ascetical practices.

Ignatius recognized that there are two spirits working on the human heart, one for good and one for bad. Closely bound, they must be separated out from each other like the strands of a rope. Ignatius developed a shrewd evaluation of motives and decisions, not taking them at face value. From his own experience he questioned: Is this actually good? What good is it bringing me? Will it be fruitful in the long run? Is it exploiting some weakness or bringing genuine growth? His system of discernment combined affective "heart" knowledge (feelings and emotions) with rational "head" knowledge (using all relevant information), making for a very sophisticated system that uses human strengths and guards against inevitable weaknesses.

Alone in the cave, this helped me to not beat myself up about the fall on the road or the notion of "failing" the walk. My desire for success, happy endings, and achievement was being purged once again. I was reevaluating my walk in terms of God's desire for me. Just like Ignatius, I was being "refined" of unhelpful tendencies and invited to be more at peace with my injury, incompletion of the walk, and the consolations I had received. I needed to be free of these small compulsions and addictions to live closer to God. The vexing issue of expectations was central: I had suffered due to my bringing high hopes based on my past Camino walks. I needed to "let go" here to be free to accept my reality. I was caught in my desire that it all be exactly like the last time, or better. I remembered only the best bits of my previous walks, of course, and was holding God to an imaginary deal whereby things would go my way. When that didn't happen, I got upset and frustrated. Obviously, I had to drop my expectations. Something significant was happening within me, but it was paradoxical and not immediately evident.

I was so busy writing down my reflections that I cut it tight for the train and had to rush down to the station. I had to jog the last 200 yards with my backpack, not easy with an injured knee. Sweaty and flustered, I collapsed into the cool air-conditioned train. The announcements of the upcoming stations were not working, so I had to keep an eye out and sit near the exit with my gear ready. In a somber mood, I listened to U2's "Song for Someone" on my phone, which seemed appropriate.[85] It was the paradox of "the light you can't always see," that there was a bigger context and plan that wasn't immediately evident.

When we arrived at the Plaça de Catalunya station in Barcelona, a guy with a bike got off in front of me, and I trailed up the platform behind him, not having to worry about people bumping into me. Walking out into the blazing sun was like entering an arena of grand architecture and consequence, and many people thronged the sidewalks. My mobile went off. It was my Jesuit friend, Enric, checking where I was. In a few minutes I arrived at his community house, and it felt like a homecoming. That night, we had a long chat on the roof terrace, the coolest place in the building. The other community members joined us for dinner there. We talked until dark and I could no longer see; my Spanish was going downhill, and I realized I was ready for sleep.

---

85. See the playlist at the end of the book for details on this song and others mentioned.

12

THE DIVINE ARCHITECT

I woke from a troubled sleep, sucking for air. Heat hung in the air like a heavy blanket. My claustrophobic dreams receded like a turgid tide, and a solitary fan fluttered uselessly in the window. A vivid dream that an old friend had deceived me continued to resonate during my ablutions. Things had seemed fine in our friendship initially, but there was a falsehood that revealed itself only too late. Was there a message in this for me, some truth I had to face up to? I felt that my dodgy knee and the city's oppressive heat were alerting me to a dangerous deception. I could no longer pretend that everything was all right on this Camino.

I had a long, slow breakfast in the community room, where windows were flung open high over a humming Barcelona. I was in no hurry, taking time to chat with the older Jesuits who, like me, had surfaced late from slumber. Later, in the airless chapel, I reluctantly opened the morning prayer app on my phone.[86] Once I got into the prayer, I began to hear the words differently. "Lord, open my lips" meant handing all my injury over to God, handing over control, and asking for forgiveness, and cleansing—a new start. "Your love is better than life" seemed to point to the fragility of life, the vulnerability

---

86. When I find myself resistant to prayer and to going inward, Ignatius recommends holding to my normal routine and resolutions, focusing my efforts to pray as I can't afford to compromise this key support (SE 319).

of the human body, and the essential nature of love that transcends everything. To "give light to those who walk in darkness" spoke to me directly, knowing exactly what it's like to stumble and fall in the darkness. Could God really shine a light into the darkness surrounding the injury and its uncertainty?

After prayer, it was time for me to make plans to return home. I spent an hour checking flights and options before opting to fly directly to Belfast, even though it cost more. It seemed a wise decision. I had given up on saving money as a priority. In the two days left on this pilgrimage, I had to decide what to do here in Barcelona.

Barcelona was an important place for St. Ignatius. It acted as a jumping-off point for other trips but particularly was a place of learning and discernment. In 1523, a devout but impetuous Ignatius traveled to Jerusalem convinced that his life's mission was to be close to Christ in the "holy places." But to his consternation, he was expelled by the authorities, and he found himself back in Barcelona starting from scratch, figuring out what God wanted from him. Reality had crashed his plans. His great inspirations had turned to dust, and he had to figure out what everything meant. His autobiography tells us that he realized that being in Jerusalem was not God's will for him: "He kept wondering what he ought to do, and finally he was inclined toward spending some time in studies in order to help souls."[87] This was a much more modest but strategic plan, and it illustrates growing wisdom on Ignatius's part. He remained in Barcelona and studied Latin grammar and other basics for nearly two years. He was a thirty-four-year-old adult learning among boys. This was all a prerequisite for university and undoubtedly an exercise in humility and trust in a greater plan. Outside his studies, he dedicated the remainder of his time to prayer, penance (including deliberately making holes in the

---

87. Joseph N. Tylenda, SJ, *A Pilgrim's Journey: The Autobiography of Ignatius of Loyola* (Collegeville, MN: Liturgical Press, 1991), No. 50.

soles of his shoes), and begging. He was to learn a lot about the workings of God during this time, especially discerning genuine signs of God's presence.

When he found it difficult to concentrate in the classroom because of the continual fresh and wondrous insights that kept him up late at night, Ignatius realized that these apparent spiritual intuitions were actually distractions from his studies and not of God. It was the unveiling of a deeper and paradoxical wisdom for Ignatius that allowed him to successfully finish his studies and incorporate these crucial insights into the *Spiritual Exercises*. *There is some relevance here for me*, I thought. My inflated expectations for my Camino experience had become a source of distress and inner disturbance. My "great" memories from the previous walks were destroying my current peace of mind.

Back in the Jesuit residence, I figured that extensive trekking around the city to see other Ignatian sites would not be a good idea. But, the church adjacent to the residence contained the actual sword St. Ignatius had used as a soldier and presented to Our Lady of Montserrat in his all-night vigil. The receptionist indicated to me the back entrance into the church, and I picked my way through building supplies and dusty storerooms to get to the door.

The Sacred Heart church (Sagrad Cor de Jesús), with its neo-Byzantine style, had a subdued mood. The high altar and sanctuary shimmered gold in the dim light. The architect, Joan Martorell, had been one of Antoni Gaudí's teachers. I headed straight for the side altar, where I found the sword of Ignatius that I had heard so much about. It was very low key, mounted in a dark bronze display case. I had to search for the light switch to make it spring into relief. The blade was surprisingly long and thin, and the makeshift hilt had no guard, which made it seem even longer. It was nothing like what I imagined, bland in its ordinariness. I was excited to see the two roughly hewn *Y*s in the blade, signifying *Yñigo Yañez*, Ignatius's name before his conversion. I marveled at this and that it had eventually found its way back to the Jesuits here in the church on Casp Street. In its presence, I wondered what dark deeds it had been involved in and what had notched its blade. Then I thought of Ignatius: How hard had it been for him to hand his sword over and walk away to a new life? How much did his previous swash-buckling lifestyle and expectations work against his decision to accept God's plan? My wonder eventually turned to self-reflection: What parts of my life did I have to hand over to start anew? What were the blocks that kept me from God? Certainly life had been very heavy for me back at home, and I was aware of a growing unease with some aspects of the bereavement work.

Later, taking refuge in an air-conditioned café, I reflected on this key relic of St. Ignatius. It was a powerful symbol of conversion from one way of life to another: a weapon of violence decommissioned and given new meaning in a dramatic vigil of arms. This latter ritual, normally signifying entry into knighthood, saw Ignatius switching allegiance over to Christ, his new Lord, a new following of a nonvio-lent leader. Significantly, the central dynamic remained the same: the deeply personal and loving devotion of a knight for his lord, but the living of it was radically different. It was this love of Christ and the intimate relationship with God that would come to define Ignatius's faith. That closeness and affection was what I desired most. Just then, outside, I saw a blind man with a white cane and a woman with a crutch walking arm in arm past the window. It struck me that there was inner blindness in my life, things that kept me from a new close-ness and intimacy with Christ. The idea of being afflicted for life with a bad knee, as Ignatius was, didn't seem like too much of a cost for getting insight and perspective. I felt I was close to some revelation that as of yet eluded me.

A day to kill and a desire to see something uplifting settled me on a visit to the famous church designed by Antoni Gaudí: La Basílica de la Sagrada Família (Holy Family). I had been there on my novitiate pilgrimage in 1994 but had heard recently that the church, still unfinished after many decades, was now even more outstanding. I needed some good news, some completion or redemption, a high note to finish off this trip. A quick search on the Internet revealed a convenient metro route, and thirty minutes later, I was exiting the station at Gaudí's ecclesial masterpiece.

I came out opposite the Nativity façade to find the pavement was thronged with crowds admiring and photographing this intricate entrance from afar. The classic statues and faces of the birth of Jesus are set into a rich, organic tapestry of rocks, animals, birds, and trees. The figures seemed to spring to life. It was the first façade completed for this church, and I remembered having seen it twenty years before. Excited, I made my way to the entrance, anxious to see the interior.

Unfortunately, on entry, I was swept along by hordes of tourists from every continent who seemed voraciously intent on capturing everything on their digital devices immediately. This digital mob was in constant movement and generating so much noise that there was no chance for stillness or contemplation. This was incongruent with what I thought was one of the most beautiful churches on earth, a place begging for depth and delay. Escape was to sit out of the traffic in the seats in the nave with the headphones of the audio guide on and my gaze turned upward.

Nothing could have prepared me for the visual feast that awaited. The heavenly light lifted my soul, a rich suffusion of myriad colors that spilled from unseen windows. The deep hues and diffused light created a sense of awe, inviting prayer and worship. It was like a clearing in a forest. The soaring, tailored columns and impossibly high ceiling canopy expressed through built form the existence of higher things. Putting this Camino experience in perspective, I was still alive, able to walk and move, and especially to feel and to pray. I felt that the deeper meaning to this unfortunate walk would eventually be revealed to me. In fact, I felt that my visit to Gaudí's basilica was a moment of light, of transient revelation, in what had been an extended period of darkness.

In this light, I slowly moved through the rest of Gaudí's radiant jewel, astounded by its great beauty. Molded from stone were the great Christian doctrines of creation, redemption, Nativity, Passion, and Resurrection. This was not some reenactment of distant history but a life enfleshed in sandstone, granite, and concrete. The preeminence of nature was everywhere. Pillars and supports mimicked the design of trees, thickly rooted from below and branching up into leaves and flowers.

Stepping out through the Passion façade was a shocking contrast to the inner harmony. I knew immediately that I had transitioned into a harsh desert of stone and hard edges, the very surfaces deeply pockmarked. The bleakness of Jesus' experience on the cross was etched, chiseled, and wrenched out of dull gray stone. This was a monument to apparent hopelessness and inhumanity, a hard place to be. I felt the desolation viscerally: the exposure of wounds, suffering, and an innate repulsion. It was too close to the bone, too reminiscent of failure. This was a place where God felt absent, where humanity was dashed on the rocks, and hope forsaken.[88] It was like the harsh reality of stripped-down nakedness and exposure. Failure, suffering, and death bled out on a boneyard. It was an uncomfortable reminder of my own limits and mortality. Needing to escape, I reentered through the huge bronze doors back into the suffused interior light. Upon reentry, the words carved in relief into the bronze doors, extracted from the Gospels, caught my attention. In a sea of gray-green, the highly polished letters

---

88. The experience of Jesus feeling forsaken, knowing the power of darkness, and feeling the absence of God is often downplayed in the Passion. Raymond E. Brown, *The Death of the Messiah, From Gethsemane to the Grave, A Commentary on the Passion Narratives in the Four Gospels*. Anchor Bible Reference Library 2 (New York: Geoffrey Chapman, 1994), 1046–47.

of the name "*Jesus*" shone like the sun. For some reason this little detail, a splash of color, gave me great hope, so I asked a stranger to take my picture. I went inside for a last, lingering look. I had spent most of a day inside a sculpted forest, and though consoled, I had been shaken by the experience of the Passion façade.

Antoni Gaudí was born in 1852, in Reus, Catalonia, south of Barcelona on the Mediterranean coast. He was the youngest of five children born to his father, Francesc, and his mother, Antònia, both children of coppersmiths. As a youth, he suffered from poor health. He had rheumatism and misguidedly used vegetarianism and severe fasts to deal with it. The restrictions on his mobility isolated him from his peers, and he developed a fascination with nature and devout faith.

He showed an early interest in architecture and went to study in Barcelona around 1870. Gaudí's deep appreciation for his homeland and pride in his Mediterranean heritage had a huge influence on his architecture and design. After graduation, Gaudí's first designs were in the contemporary Victorianism, but he soon developed his own style, integrating Gothic features, Moorish influences, art nouveau, and organic designs from nature. The way he animated surfaces with patterns of brick, stone, or ceramic tiles reflected an Eastern influence.

Gaudí's fame as an architect grew. Seven of his buildings in Barcelona are listed by UNESCO as World Heritage Sites, but it was the Basilica of the Sagrada Familia that has come to define his architectural legacy more than any other design. After 1910, he devoted himself exclusively to it and took up residence in its workshop. Gaudí himself was fond of comparing the Sagrada Família to the Catalan mountains and specifically to the unique geology of Montserrat. When he was killed in a tram accident in 1926, he was mistaken for a homeless *beggar* after having let his appearance go. The basilica was consecrated by Benedict XVI on November 7, 2010, while still under construction. The Pope's homily spoke of the church as reflecting "a visible sign of the invisible God, to whose glory these spires rise like arrows pointing towards absolute light"[89]—a testimony to finding God in the design of form and light.

Reflecting in a café after my visit, I was savoring this exquisite experience of liquid stone. I hadn't expected the drama of nature and humanity in inanimate matter, the concrete embodiment of sinews and tissues, to be quite so immediate and raw. It seemed to me that the doctrine of the Incarnation, of God among us in the world, was particularly present in this architectural icon of theology. Known as the "Church of the Poor," it was designed for ordinary humans, especially those less well-off. I was grateful for Gaudí's vision and dedication, and for a new consciousness about my injury and how it bound me to the cross and the experience of suffering. My experience exposed the truth of who I was, stripping away pretensions. In small, human ways, I was partaking in the sufferings of Jesus, which helped me make sense of and relativize my own struggles. I was now ready to go home and face whatever medical challenges lay ahead. My right knee throbbed and brought me back to my reality. It confirmed my decision to go home to get an answer to the mysterious pain.

---

89. You can read Pope Benedict's entire homily here: www.vatican.va/content/benedict-xvi/en/homilies/2010/documents/ hf_ben-xvi_hom_20101107_barcelona.html.

13
BACK TO BLACK

At loose ends for the evening, I had a look for a nearby movie theater. I knew a well-chosen film could sometimes yield great insights; while doing the Spiritual Exercises as a novice, I had gotten a major understanding of the Passion from a Hollywood movie.[90] I hoped for some similar spiritual impetus that would shed some light on my current situation. I saw that *Amy*, a British documentary about the singer Amy Winehouse, was playing at a cinema close to the Jesuit house. Having just missed the five o'clock show, I would have to wait for two hours for the next one, but I had a strong sense this was a movie I had to see. I passed the time watching the feats of fearless teenage riders against a backdrop of colorful graffiti at a nearby skate park. When I got into the cinema, the screening was in an old-style wood paneled box room with wing-backed seats and a dubious smell, but once the lights dimmed, I was transported. The opening credits faded, and on came Amy Winehouse's life.

---

90. I had watched *The Bodyguard* (1992), where the self-sacrificing love of the bodyguard explained Christ's personal love for me: "No one has greater love than this, to lay down one's life for one's friends" (John 15:13). Film and television act powerfully on the imagination as pathways to uncover God's presence in the world. J. Pungente and M. Williams, *Finding God in the Dark: Taking the Spiritual Exercises of St. Ignatius to the Movies* (Ottawa: Novalis, 2004).

The movie was very personal and intimate, to the point of being exploitative: everything about her life was garishly revealed. The story was of a sweet, awkward Jewish teenager who had a God-given voice that propelled her rapidly to stardom, drugs, dysfunction, and, ultimately, death. Her unique voice and original songs eclipsed her ordinary London upbringing and quickly outgrew her motley cast of friends and handlers. The psychological cracks, cumulative consequences of bad decisions, and nefarious people who orchestrated her downfall gradually converged. Remarkably, she was able to use the misery and pain of her personal experience to craft some beautiful songs. But it wasn't long before the demons began to dictate, the drugs showed up, and the circling vultures began to pick her apart. The reel flickered into darkness, a life wrung dry, a songbird silenced, and *Amy* was over.

Alone, I cried in the dark over a wasted life and talent. The tragedy that unfolded wasn't inevitable; Amy's life was salvageable. She had been betrayed, especially by those closest to her, and was unable to manage her own unresolved darkness and pain. It was painful for me to watch—pure desolation—how the machinations of evil wove a slick web of manipulation, half truths, and lies. Amy went into meltdown in the full glare of publicity, many of her associates and family choosing not to see her suffering but to "follow the money." Eventually, the light within her was extinguished; her heart couldn't bear it any longer. It seemed to tap into some of my own desolation and emptiness; I was bereft.

Born in 1983 in London, Amy Winehouse was influenced by her grandmother Cynthia and started singing young. Her father, Mitch Winehouse, was a taxi driver, and her mother, Janis, was a pharmacist. They separated in 1992, when Amy was just nine years old, and later she cited this event as pivotal. Winehouse was allegedly expelled from school twice by the age of fourteen. She started to write music around that time, and thanks to a series of fortuitous events, got a contract with Island/Universal Records and subsequently a publishing deal with EMI.

Ironically, her reported drinking, drug use, and weight loss were the collective emotional crucible that fueled her writing of the multiple-award-winning album *Back to Black*. In 2007 Amy got engaged to Blake Fielder-Civil. Their tragic and often violent romance was to be the inspiration for much of her songwriting. After several spells of rehab (the theme of her best-selling single), she seemed poised for a comeback in 2009. Unfortunately, addiction and her emotional issues took an enormous toll on her health. She was pronounced dead in her London home due to alcohol poisoning on July 23, 2011.

I was the last one to leave as the cleaners arrived in the theater. There was an unpleasant aftertaste of witnessing evil at work. I thought of how many good things, including Amy's life, had been destroyed for very sordid and shortsighted motives. More than anything, the entertainment industry and culture were exposed as exploitative and uncaring, a keen example of structural or social sin. No one really cared enough to make an intervention, to get her help to address her demons, or to prevent her from going onstage drunk or drugged. I felt strongly that darkness of soul, turmoil, and disturbance that Ignatius must have intended to define by the term *desolation*. I felt drained and desolate, overexposed to devastation. I needed to move myself back into the light, to act against the pervasive negativity.[91] I set out for the Jesuit home on Zamora Street.

The desolation spoke to my own despair over a "failed" Camino experience. Unlike my previous light-filled pilgrimage walks, I seemed to have gotten nothing significant from this one. Rather, I could feel the temptation to fall prey to rumination, to open old wounds ("I always get injured or sick"), and to be overpowered by negativity and inertia. So powerful was the negative pull that I had to use some of the Ignatian rules for combating desolation to insulate myself.[92] I knew from previous experience that anxiety, sadness, and negative thinking were the seductive seeds of discontent that, if given full rein, would flourish and overpower me, as they had with Amy. I knew that there was something significant in the movie for me, something about the passivity and inevitability about Amy's story. What was it I needed to do in order to avoid the catastropic effects of desolation?[93]

My first priority when I arrived back at the Barcelona Jesuit house was to reconnect and reengage with some of the community, and then I had a time of prayer and reflection in the chapel to "recharge" on positivity, perspective, and light, even though I knew to avoid making any big decisions while I was temporarily going through a rough spot. The challenge was to identify and address the sources of desolation. I had no idea what this could mean for me, if it was something to do with the walk or some situation back at

---

91. Amy and those around her go from one excess to another, making a series of bad decisions; things gradually get worse, ending with her death. This is the dynamic of the bad spirit who takes over, encounters no resistance, and wreaks havoc (SE 314, 335).

92. Remain firm in commitments, don't change course, reapply ourselves to practices that work (SE 313–27).

93. In a positive sense, the unease or disturbing nature of desolation is essentially a "wake-up" call to react against isolation and immobility, to address the situation and take action (SE 317–322).

home. Right then, though, it was a time for battening down the hatches and riding out the storm.

My spirit agitated, I didn't sleep well that night. I had a very disquieting, half-remembered "falling" dream that hung about me in the morning. I read it as a warning about passivity and a stimulus to act. It was a sharp reminder about my own health situation.

With some time to spare before the flight, I had a strong urge to go to Mass in the Sagrada Familia to reconnect with the light. Morning Mass was on in the neo-Renaissance crypt of the famous basilica, and arriving late, sweaty, and breathless, I was unable to concelebrate the Mass as a priest, which had been my hope. I struggled to find gratitude just to be there, to be alive, and to experience the presence of Christ in this sacred ritual in a most inspiring location. I remembered Amy while I was there, praying for her and giving thanks for the insights from her story. Far removed from the hordes of tourists above, the crypt was a quiet refuge of hushed words, awe, and mystery. There was a special blessing at the end of Mass for people visiting for the first time and for babies, which was very moving—a newborn named Lourdes, a man from Boston, a woman from Colombia, another from Croatia, and myself. It was the perfect pilgrim blessing for me, an unfinished pilgrim in an unfinished cathedral.

Tiredness suddenly set in, and I just wanted to get home as fast and as painlessly as possible. I dragged myself back to the Jesuit house to pack and say goodbye to my friend, Enric, and soon, I was ready for the bus journey to the airport.

The massive Barcelona Airport, one of the busiest in Europe, is not somewhere you want to be when you are not feeling well. Lights, announcements, trolleys, and speed walkers abound to place one under constant pressure. A slow limp was my top speed, and I held myself apart from the frenetic rush as a crucial survival trick. The word *failure* was trying to impress itself on my consciousness on this journey home. I understood only too well the tyranny of perfection, the allergy to making mistakes, and the illusion of success. But it was hard not to judge myself or to anticipate the judgments of others based on the evidence of this visibly broken gait. An injury could be liberating too, I realized; Ignatius's faith story of abandoning a fanciful career to live a radically different life was directly due to his injury. It was a moment of painful catharsis; he was forced to abandon the superficial life and live entirely from grace and providence. The insight was that grace could operate through failure. I was heartened by this thought, though the implications of what this might mean for my life and ministry still eluded me.

On the way to the gate, TV screens looped ubiquitous media images of refugees fleeing through Eastern Europe and crawling through barbed wire at borders with pitifully few possessions. I felt for them fighting the fight of their lives, totally committed to survival and hoping against hope. Seeing those images put my journey into perspective. I could see Christ's Passion in these images; a suffering and frail humanity was exposed, with violence and exploitation seeming to dominate. The prayer of Jesus' abandonment and paradoxical trust came to me: "My God, my God, why have you forsaken me?" (Matthew 27:46). I needed to trust that God is in these situations, even mine, and that good can come out of the desperate darkness. Aboard the plane, I kept praying to escape my own bitter emotions and the seeming negativity of this flawed walking project.

Arrival at the Sanctuary of Loyola, Basque Country, birthplace of St Ignatius and start of the Ignatian Camino. The sanctuary's basilica (with dome) can be seen in the background.

The first stage of the Ignatian Camino, Loyola–Zumarraga, passes through tunnels on an old railway line.

The Hermitage of Santa María ("La Antigua"), outside Zumarraga, where Ignatius reputedly prayed

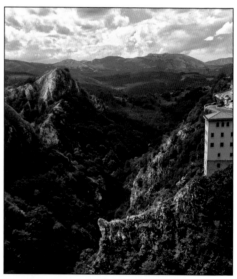

View from Franciscan Sanctuary of Arantzazu, set in the Aizkorri mountains

Getting treatment after the fall at the medical centre in Legazpi

Sheep in a misty Aizkorri-Aratz Natural Park near the hermitage on the Urbia plains

Deep mud on the Araia–Alda path en route to the mountain pass over the Entzia mountains

The main retablo of the Church of Nuestra Señora de la Asunción, Navarrete, La Rioja

Statue of the Virgin Mary reputedly restored by Ignatius, Church of Nuestra Señora de la Asunción, Navarrete, La Rioja

Posing between Camino statues outside Logroño, where the author had to abandon the walk

The view from the Benedictine monastery Santa Maria de Montserrat into Catalonia

Our Lady of Montserrat, the "Black Madonna" and child in the basilica at Montserrat

The famous "cave" or "grotto" in Manresa where St. Ignatius reputedly wrote the *Spiritual Exercises*

Posing at the portal of the Passion façade, Gaudí's Basílica de la Sagrada Familia, Barcelona

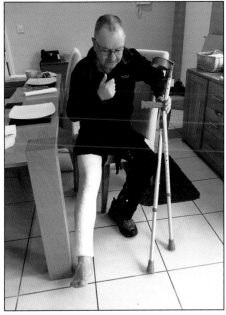

Inspecting the newly applied cast in the Jesuit community in Belfast

Travelling to Manchester to give a talk on the Camino

The author performing a Bono impersonation, "One," Magis 2016, Poland

14

THE GOOD DOCTOR

The airplane swooped low over Belfast Lough, its gray chop reflecting a leaden sky. It had been an uncomfortable flight; the rigid sitting position kept my knee bent and created an acute throb. I remembered a different journey some four years previously when I touched down ecstatic from my Camino experience, bursting to get home and share the good news with friends and family. The dull thump and screech of touchdown was a harsh reminder of how different this attempt had been. It was hard not to keep making comparisons with my previous experience, though I knew this one was fraught with elements of failure.[94] I had nothing to show for my walk except a painful knee (a mysterious ailment), a series of medical interventions that was far from inspiring, and my certificate for completion of the Ignatian Camino, which I had barely qualified for, having just about made the required hundred kilometers, or sixty-two miles. *It wasn't supposed to end like this*, I reflected gloomily, as I limped down the steps in some pain.

---

94. In a real sense, expectations become idols that dominate our thinking and take away our peace, necessitating a reality check to deal with them. Tim Muldoon, *The Ignatian Workout: Daily Spiritual Exercises for a Healthy Faith* (Chicago: Loyola Press, 2004), 11–12.

Emerging into the crowded arrivals terminal, I looked hopefully around. Normally, I wouldn't expect anyone to meet me, but this time the lack of a friendly face hit me harder than usual. There was nothing left but to board a bus for the city center and make my way to St. Anne's Cathedral, where I had started this journey three weeks prior and which was now my finishing point. Off the bus, I wandered through Belfast on the way to St. Anne's. I longed to meet a familiar face, to have a providential encounter, but there was none. With some considerable frustration, I questioned where God was now, when I really needed support. How could God let me down? Especially when I had tried to get it all so right.

Hoping to see the friendly shop assistant I had met before, I entered an outdoor shop where I had bought some hiking gear before the trip. I needed someone to acknowledge what I had done. But the woman wasn't there. Instead, it was a different salesman who failed to notice my backpack and hiking gear and asked me how he could help. Disappointed at his lack of perception, I impulsively cast around for some pretext. My eye fell on the sale rack, and I grabbed a thermal top, even though I didn't really need it. It was a visceral reaction, seeking warmth against all the cold I felt invading my being. Before I knew it, I was buying something I didn't really need, an uncomfortable feeling. It was compensation for the inner unease I felt, which needed to be addressed.[95] Stuffing my purchase into the backpack was a cold comfort, and my spirit weighed heavier than ever.

A short time later, I walked up the steps of St. Anne's Cathedral, retracing my steps from the beginning of this endeavor. This was to be my ritual of closure for the trip, but even this was complicated. I

---

95. Going against my deeper instincts of discernment and weighing decisions, I was acting impulsively and against my better judgment. The resultant uncomfortable feeling was what Ignatius would call desolation, God's emotional warning sign that I was going in the wrong direction (SE 317, 318).

asked the man at the desk for a stamp in my Ignatian Camino pilgrim passport, a Camino staple, but he didn't understand my request and sent me to the gift shop. Resignedly, I sat in a pew, and my eyes travelled up to the Trinity window in the sanctuary, high above the altar. I remembered seeing this window in all its glory as the resurrection some weeks ago—that seemed like a different age, "the time before the fall." Now my eyes were drawn to the darker colors below, the red, black, and cool blue that made up the crown of thorns. The pain and discomfort from my fall was making me see things differently; God was working through this somehow. From this sense of aloneness and perceived abandonment I had a new understanding of the cross experience for Jesus. Previously, it had seemed like a good act: Jesus plays dead and then comes smiling back to life. I really needed to believe and understand that Jesus had gone through the mill. He had really experienced the limits of human suffering. His "triumphal entry" into Jerusalem hadn't lasted; even for him the well of consolation and faith had suddenly dried up, and, shockingly, Jesus was left feeling bereft and betrayed by God. Somehow, it helped me to remember the depth of Jesus' isolation and bitter failure on the cross but also the promise of the Resurrection that was concealed within it. I was only sensing a minute fraction of this experience in this cathedral, but it was food for thought and the seed of some hope.

Limping home the last uphill mile, I was in a daze, uncaring and apathetic. I could barely talk to my Jesuit friends about what had happened—my situation sounded so lame and worthless. Drained, I fell into bed for another night of pulsing pain and broken sleep. The following day was one of headaches and fatigue. The temptation was to just lie in bed. I knew this was not going to help me in my goal to resolve the underlying problem, but the pain and tiredness conspired to make me rest and do nothing for the day.[96]

The next day, steeling myself against the inertia and negative thoughts, I limped up to my local clinic. My heart fell to be greeted by an intern, cheery and bright but looking young and inexperienced. After a cursory examination, I was told once again (for the third time now) that it was probably overuse after the original injury and just needed time, rest, and anti-inflammatories. Fighting a rising resentment, I asked her to double check if it could not be something else, explaining the fall and the presence of a persistent pain. I was surprised that she didn't send me for an X-ray. There was nothing evident, she assured me, and it was with a mixture of frustration and despair that I hobbled back home. Would there be no end to this? Was there something I was missing here? Was it something I would have to live with? The not knowing was frustrating and soul destroying, and it was hard not to feel helpless in the face of all this.

I had held out for an eleventh-hour deliverance, but it hadn't come; I felt cheated, bruised, and raw. Now, washed up in Belfast, I was worse off than before, with a busted knee. The tide had gone out on my original 2011 Camino experience, and the wonderful afterglow had evaporated with the fall on this one. *Had this all been a bad idea?* I wondered. *Had I been misguided?* In my bitter ruminations, I was left wondering, *Where is God in all this?*

Passing the Presbyterian church on my way home, Jesus' final words popped into my head: *"My God, my God, why have you forsaken me?"* (Matthew 27:46). It was a strange thing for him to say on the cross but especially shocking in the context of a father-son relationship. Jesus is quoting Psalm 22 here, a prayer emphasizing faith in darkness, but there is no getting away from this shocking dynamic of the father seeming absent. It would be cruel to abandon one's son at

---

96. In Ignatian language, I had to act against (*agere contra*) the forces that kept me away from a genuinely life-giving solution, even if it meant "short-term pain and long-term gain" (SE 13).

his darkest hour, in his greatest pain, and when he was in most need of some reassurance. Jesus didn't know, couldn't have known, that the Resurrection was just around the corner. He had to grit his teeth and endure the pain and fear of death like any human. Passing through a trial and experiencing the absence of God, I too needed to find this deeper meaning in my experience.[97]

Close to home, leaves were falling in the Waterworks park, signaling the change of season. Autumn was underway. The image of Christ suffering the agony of those last hours, not knowing, and feeling abandoned stayed with me. He had to hand it all over and pray for light in the midst of terrible darkness. Similarly, I needed to give it all up to God, not hold anything back, and pray the same words that Jesus uses on the cross: "Father, into your hands I commend my spirit" (Luke 23:46). I had to trust that in God's time some light would come. Again, for Jesus it wasn't in the way that he might have wanted it: "not my will but yours be done" (Luke 22:42). But, through his experience of dying came a rise to new life. And although my situation was miniscule in comparison, there would be no shortcuts in this process for me, either—I would have to pass through the storm to get to the calm. The great irony was that God appears to work most powerfully in the darkness. So, like Jesus, I would have to be faithful to the process, even when feeling abandoned, to get to some resolution or "resurrection" experience. It happened for Jesus, and I had to believe it would happen again for me. I watched a swan thunder down the lake on a long takeoff. Faith was hoping against hope, hanging on in the face of suffering, and believing that God was in this disabling experience somewhere.[98]

---

97. I remembered this from the thirty-day retreat of the Spiritual Exercises, as part of my Jesuit training, in the third week—the challenge of being with Christ in his Passion and witnessing the suffering that he endured for me (SE 190–209).

As the days wore into weeks, my knee continued to oscillate between pain and relief. Grimly determined, I made an appointment with a physiotherapist whom I had used before. There had to be an answer to this painful mystery. Two days later, I was in her office. She began the examination carefully and systematically worked through the range of movements, testing the flexibility of the knee. It was strange how the pain seemed to vanish under examination, like an elusive rare animal. However, she did spend a long time working the kneecap before finally announcing that there was something wrong with its positioning and that the muscles around it weren't working properly. She attempted to strap the kneecap in position but then thought better of it. Finally, she proclaimed: "I don't want to touch this; it would be better to go to the hospital's Accident and Emergency and get it X-rayed. Until we see what's going on underneath, it's impossible to know what the problem is or how to treat it." I could have hugged her, I was so overjoyed to get a possible diagnosis, but I held myself back. She recommended I go first thing in the morning.[99]

The next morning, ever the optimist, I cycled down to Belfast's Mater hospital and settled in for what was to be a long wait. When I finally did get called, a Somali doctor examined me and his quirky sense of humor warmed the minimalist cubicle. He sent me to the X-ray department. Ever hopeful, I was anticipating losing the limp, maybe that same day. In the waiting room I met a young man I knew; he walked on a stick and was in for a routine scan. As I heard him describe his journey back from near death, his coping with severe injury, and his unshakeable faith, I was simultaneously taken aback and impressed.

98. Finding God in all things is easy when things are going well, but faced with the pain of a tough situation, it demands a lot of faith, courage, and practice at reflection on experience (SE 43).
99. X-rays are normally authorized by a general practicioner, but as I had already had no success with that route, this "emergency" approach was the best bet.

*Five years previously, Mick had barely survived a major traffic acci-
dent, in which he sustained a traumatic brain injury. A promising aca-
demic, he was cycling to work when he was hit by a car. Such was
the extent of his head injuries that he almost didn't survive. He has no
memory of the accident whatsoever and only came back to consciousness some months later. He struggled to come to terms with what had
happened and to accept the medically imposed limitations.*

*The doctors held scant hope for any significant recovery of mobil-
ity. He made little progress initially, but later with much more encour-
agement, he abandoned his wheelchair and was able to walk unaided.
Much of his life now is a continuous reminder of the terrible accident
that left him with the traumatic brain injury.*

*Extraordinarily, Mick sees himself as having been richly blessed
with the gift of life in the first place and then the joy of surviving and
recovering from a serious accident, so he wants to communicate that
blessedness to others. He bears no trace of rancor toward the car driver.
His relationship with God has deepened through these hard struggles
and is developing. He is able to find God in all things, even these most
challenging of things: the limitations, the degradations, the long lonely
bedridden hours. In his words: "The Lord carries me through even this
much darkness. I know well my vulnerability, my limits. I marvel at
my survival and the long silent recovering, this continuing on." Mick
has recently finished an MA and is optimistic about getting back to
writing again, his great love.*

The X-ray room was simple, all shiny steel and protruding cables. The
technologist had me crouch in different positions to capture images
of my knee. After another wait downstairs, I was called in to see the
same doctor around lunchtime. "It's a fractured kneecap," he said, and
showed it to me on the monitor. It was so obvious; how could three
doctors have missed it?! It was such a relief to finally see it in black
and white, to know that I hadn't imagined it and that there was a
solution. I felt vindicated. It explained a lot. The doctor continued to
crack jokes as reality set in; I had walked for two weeks on a fractured

knee. Unsure of the next step, I was charmed by this doctor who had been my savior, my deliverance.

I was floored to discover that he was ordering a full leg cast, and he disappeared to make the necessary arrangements. Suddenly my phone bleeped to remind me that I had someone waiting for me back in my house who had come from Dublin for spiritual direction. Weighing up the decision, I figured I had waited over a month to get this diagnosis, so postponing the application of the cast for another hour or two wouldn't make much difference. I asked the doctor if I could delay the cast while I attended to this urgent meeting, which he allowed. So, I phoned a friend for a ride and was back at the house in minutes. A quick coffee, and I was sitting with the person who was coming to meet me, my leg propped on a cushion to immobilize the newly discovered fracture. I was possessed of a new Zen-like calm, greatly consoled that the "demon" injury had been exposed, and I turned my attention to my guest.

Arriving back in the hospital later, I took my seat among a variety of patients, silently counting my blessings about all the good that had happened today.[100] I looked around at some of my waiting companions: Right next to me a woman complained of blinding headaches and looked grim and pained; a young footballer still in his kit was helped into a chair, having injured his hand in a match mere minutes before; I even saw a local TV personality enter with his son. I was really struck by how anyone could end up there regardless of background, class, or status. I saw another older man wheeled in on a bed, eyes open, obviously in some distress, and unable to speak. My impatience melted away as I became aware of where I was, a melting pot of humanity from all walks of life, and I greatly admired the medical

---

100. This was a form of the Examen prayer, of focusing on the positive and the gifts you have received; it breaks the cycle of negativity or self-pity that it is easy for some to fall victim to (SE 43).

staff who were daily ministers of health and healing. I was grateful to the National Health Service who provided this huge service free of charge.

After some hours of waiting (I had now been there over eight hours in total), I was called to have the plaster cast applied. Again, the Somali doctor was there with that irrepressible humor, and I felt a real warmth for him and his demeanor. I could feel whatever resentment I had against the failures of the previous doctors melting away. He gravely indicated that he was going to have to cut up the leg of my trousers to put the cast on. Brandishing a huge pair of scissors, he paused, a mischievous gleam in his eyes. He had me in stitches as he made the cut. Then, he handed me over to a nurse for the application of the cast. It was a wonderful sensory treat: the layering of the hot bandages, the sweet smell of the plaster of Paris, and the drama of seeing the cast dry to a rock-hard consistency. It seemed like total overkill having a full leg cast for such a small knee fracture, but it very much looked the part in announcing to the world that something was broken.

Then came a short demonstration on how to use crutches. I was a real rookie. Finally, I was placed in a wheelchair with my plaster-stained and shredded trousers, my new crutches clasped tightly to my chest, and brought to the door of the hospital to await a ride. That was the worst moment: Even though I was only several hundred yards from where my friend was parked, I felt the implications of the injury and cast suddenly kick in. I didn't realize to what extent I would be reliant on friends for a lot of help now. Life was going to be very different for the next few months, at least. I would have to adjust to a new reality. I asked my friend to bring my bike home for me. My optimism had betrayed me; it would be awhile before I used it again.

15
ESCAPING THE CRUTCHES

Balancing on the crutches at the top of the stairs was more than a little daunting. I tried swinging my good foot forward and down, out over the abyss, a dangerous move. I cast around for other solutions: going down on my bottom, going down backwards, or maybe not going down at all. Necessity eventually forced a solution. I let the right crutch dangle around my arm while I grasped the banister with my right hand to use as a solid anchor. This way I could swing the cast ahead down the stairs and step down. It wasn't so terrifying now; at least I had something solid to hold onto. It was a slow and ungraceful but safe descent. Things were different now. Once in the kitchen, getting breakfast was another major hurdle requiring assistance, props (a leg rest), and logistics to coordinate the arrival of all the ingredients at the same time. It was too difficult to sit at the table, so my colleagues set up a stool for me at the work top, where I could reach the fridge and most of the staples.

As a person with a (temporary) disability, I saw the house differently now. An old nineteenth-century Victorian house with high ceilings and narrow staircases, it had no facility or sympathy for injured persons. The sheer number of stairs had never struck me before, nor did I see the barrier posed by the entrance steps. Even the narrow bathrooms were clearly designed for the able bodied. In fact, seen from my new perspective, every change in level, passage, and doorway became a barrier to be managed. My new life was divided into two settings: one upstairs and another downstairs. Once down the stairs in the morning, I was confined to spending the day there before facing my summit bid back up to the bedroom in the evening. Whereas before I wouldn't think twice about heading down to the chapel for evening prayer, now once upstairs for the evening, I wouldn't consider going back down again because of what the ascent would cost me.

YouTube was indispensable in figuring out how to use crutches properly. There is a lot of technique needed to reach forward to place the crutches firmly on the ground, lift your entire body weight with your arms, swing both legs forward, land balancing on the good leg, and then begin the cycle again. I had to practice walking around the house, building up unfamiliar muscles, and getting used to making many new mistakes.

After the first couple of weeks, I was going a bit stir-crazy in the house. I wondered how Ignatius had survived his months of confinement in his room convalescing in Loyola. I decided to test my ability with the crutches in the local park, some 300 yards away. The bird life in the Waterworks was always lively, especially in autumn, a chaotic mix of swans, geese, ducks, and assorted gulls. With my arm muscles not fully up to the task, I was taken aback at how long it took me to cover the short distance. I had to stop and rest frequently. Fortunately, the only bench in the park within range was empty, and I collapsed onto it, swiveling the cast up onto the bench for comfort. It was a small accomplishment, but important. It was proof that I could get out of the house unaided, a tiny victory for independence. I celebrated just being in the air and feeling the breeze.[101]

---

101. I was being invited to see things differently, to realize that all is a gift from God, to avoid ingratitude and self-pitying introversion (SE 234–37).

A Graylag goose on the footpath ahead of me was holding one foot in the air. It had hurt it somehow and was attempting to walk on one leg, just like I [was]. Somehow it found a way of waddling that minimized the pain and kept it going forward. A "lame duck" was the phrase that came to me, the pejorative dimension of it hitting home. The goose eventually made its way back into the water, where it swam normally. I realized it was time for me to go; the cold was biting. The journey home seemed monumental; the unfamiliar pain in my arms and shoulders was shouting "Stop." Somehow, I managed to get home.

Back home in the Jesuit community, I was glad to collapse into an armchair and lift my leg on a footrest. It had been a tough but rewarding outing, a small triumph. I wasn't able to do as much as I had thought, which confirmed my limits were real. Delicate but insistent, the dull tingling pain in my knee proclaimed that something broken was slowly mending. I needed to be able to ask for help. What was unhelpful was thinking in terms of extremes. One extreme was total passivity, giving up and lying in bed, and the other was recklessly behaving as if there were no injury. The key was to live in that middle ground somewhere, finding a way through the obstacles, respecting limits but having courage.[102] I had a new respect for people who live with permanent physical, mental, or spiritual disabilities. They need much courage and tenacity to get through the day and carry out tasks most of us take for granted. As in life, and on the Camino, you cannot judge people from the outside, and it is the heart where the real journey and conversion takes place.

---

102. To make spiritual progress, a certain amount of experience, reflection, and adjustment is needed to move away from excess and find a mean or balance. Michael Ivens, SJ, *Understanding the Spiritual Exercises* (Leominster, UK: Gracewing, 1998), 218. (See also SE 13, 317, 322).

As fall wore on, however, my positive attitude and willingness to make the best of things and find balance began to wear out. I couldn't prevent a downward slide, and anger and irritability were close by. Even with my meditation and awareness practices, God seemed distant, and frustration seeped into my consciousness and relationships. I was withdrawn and sullen in the community, and even uncharacteristically sarcastic. I felt increasingly my patience wearing thin; delays or inconveniences unearthed a certain anger. *How could this have happened?* I reflected. After my last Camino in 2011, I had tried to implement various insights from living more simply to trusting in providence and being more available for others. Going back for the Ignatian Camino had seemed like a logical "top up" to underline my new lifestyle. Yet, with the ill-fated fall, events had been set in motion that brought me to this bitter impasse. I was possibly trying to replicate the past but falling into negativity and feeling far from God. I continually returned to the thought, *Where is God now?*

On top of my injury, I slid into a black pit emotionally and spiritually. The process of disability was dragging me down to the point of questioning my faith. I was resentful because I didn't want to be here, didn't want to be experiencing this decay, my frailty and neediness, and it all felt unfair. As yet, I didn't have any clear perspective or insight that helped me understand this process. Getting worked up in my room, I happened to glance out the window. Seeing a man power down the street in a wheelchair brought me to my senses. I had been immobilized in feeling sorry for myself; I had so much to be grateful for. I needed to jolt myself into the present, leave the past behind. My knee fracture had been diagnosed, and I was on my way to recovery. The healing process was playing itself out, and I had this final dark moment to be lived. The turmoil and restlessness I identified as "desolation," an interior spiritual movement away from God that indicates a lack of faith, hope, and love. I needed to do something about it before it brought me to a worse place.

Initially, after getting the cast, I had cleared my schedule. Now, I was faced with feelings of desolation and the pressing issue of my work commitments. I couldn't walk or drive, so I would have to cancel most of them, a sobering reality. However, a Jesuit friend wisely advised me not to give up all my commitments or totally cut myself off from what was normally a great source of life and energy. I had to actively resist the temptation to let desolation win. This required some discernment. I had to acknowledge my real limitations but also identify what was still possible and doable.[103] It was clear I had to drop most of my spiritual direction work and a lot of meetings and speaking engagements that involved travel. I was in no condition for them. In the end, I decided to honor a commitment to give a workshop on suicide bereavement at the local diocesan convention in a few weeks and then lead a six-week course on prayer in the local parish. The only problem was that both required my presence at the respective venues, and I would need someone to bring me there. The other priests in my house were busy themselves, so I began to think about who else I could get for this key role. I trusted that God would provide someone.

I remembered a conversation a few weeks previously with someone who had become a friend, Patrick. I had given him a lift home several times from an evening class, and we had chatted a lot about life, faith, and the Camino de Santiago. He had shared with me his ongoing battle with alcohol and how he was trying to get his life together. He had offered to help me with my work, in clerical or administrative backup, or in any other way he could. I suddenly

---

103. A balanced decision, while respecting the limits of the situation, means finding reasonable options that avoid extremes, or over- or underdoing things (SE 15, 23, 179).

thought, *What if he was to be my driver?* I contacted him right away and was delighted to hear that he had a clean driving license, would be happy to do it, and promised to remain sober for it. I set about arranging the insurance for him to drive me in a Jesuit car.

Just a couple of weeks later, I found myself being driven by Patrick across Belfast to the diocesan convention. I was strapped into the seat, almost horizontal, with the cast extended into the footwell. From this low viewing position, I was happy to see trees and leaves, a lovely autumn unfolding. It was a welcome escape from the confines of the house, at least temporarily. The journey was a chance to get to know Patrick better as well. He filled me in on his life of some small achievements but also accidents and misfortunes. He was dealing with serious ongoing health issues; each day was a monumental struggle for him, and he fought hard to stay afloat. I found his company was the perfect preparation for my bereavement workshop.

We arrived late at the school in East Belfast, where my workshop was to take place. The foyer was thronged with priests and parishioners. As people came up to greet me, I quickly felt overwhelmed. I was feeling very vulnerable on the crutches. Eventually, I was guided to the classroom where I was to give the seminar on suicide bereavement. A feeling of being off balance or out of sorts persisted throughout the talk; nothing seemed to flow. I was really feeling the cost of this type of heavy emotional work. Feeling spent and shattered, I looked for an early opportunity to close the session. The attendees seemed to enjoy the workshop, however, but I had little sense of that in my need to get away. I was relieved to find Patrick downstairs waiting for me and was glad to fit myself into the car and his care, already anticipating getting home and into bed. It had been useful, however, to realize the limits of my abilities, how much help I needed, and how hard it was to interact with a group. I resolved to put these learnings into practice the following month at the course on prayer in the local parish.

The six-week Lenten prayer course was based on the Irish Catholic Catechism, and my job was to present it in such a way that it spoke to people's lives. Ironically, I was the one most in need of it, trying to learn how to pray and adapt to a new situation where awareness and meditation were challenging. I called it "The Prayer of the Heart," based on a homily by Pope Francis.[104] Trying to make some of the theological concepts come alive was my biggest challenge, and eventually I came up with the idea of using photos and images. The advantage was that I wouldn't have to explain as much verbally; it would be much more self-evident and hopefully more powerful. For example, I used the image of a mobile phone being charged as one way of representing prayer. Also, the iconic footprints-in-the-sand image related to the paradox of feeling abandoned by God (Deuteronomy 1:31).[105] With lots of time on my hands, I rigged up a support for my leg and spent hours preparing the presentations for the parish. It gave me a much-needed focus and occupied some of the long hours spent in my room as the days grew shorter.

What I remember most about those parish talks, however, was Patrick telling me about what was going on for him during the short journeys to and from them. Life had dealt him some hard blows: he was left with a disability by a serious accident, had been divorced, and was unemployed. He vividly described what it was to be in thrall to drink in such a way that personal history, guilt, and negativity all conspired against him. I had to hold myself back on jumping in with ready answers or glib piety (e.g., God will fix that); I sensed that he

---

104. Daily homily given by Pope Francis in Casa Santa Marta, October 8, 2013.
105. The "footprints in the sand" image shows one set of footprints on a beach. The person concerned is complaining that when they were at their lowest ebb, they felt alone walking this beach. But, God counters, "Did you not realize I was carrying you all this time?"

didn't want that from me. I was convinced that the concreteness of Ignatian spirituality would be of help to him, especially protecting himself from having his weaknesses exploited, losing freedom, and becoming overly attached, but I felt I had to go slowly.[106] Mostly, I would just listen, reverencing his story and his attempts to find a way through.

Fortunately, we got on well and understood each other, united in a common mission. Patrick connected with my brother's story. His identification with him, and by association with me, brought us closer. During one of the parish talks I gave, "Praying the Passion," I told my brother's story of struggle with his demons and my attempts to save him. Suddenly, I realized that I was delivering the lecture exclusively for Patrick, who waited at the back of the room. As I spoke of my journey of redemption, I dearly wanted him to know that the Spirit was with him in his desolation and that there was hope. My instincts as a spiritual director, so much to the fore on the Ignatian Camino, were engaged now with Patrick, but also in relation to my present situation. I felt that this same dynamic of the cross, the terrible dance between death and resurrection, was operating in Patrick's life, as it had been operating in mine. He was living his "passion" through the darkness and abandonment he felt. But Christ was closer than he or I knew, and there was a way through the morass of harsh judgment and self-condemnation.

To my chagrin, he dismissed any relevance for himself in the talk; he insisted that he was in a much more unworthy place. I was sure that something significant had happened for Patrick, but it wasn't evident yet. Certainly, he was interested in some aspects of Ignatius's life story: redeeming an unworthy life, the divine present in the messiness

---

106. Being free means not being under any inordinate attachment or addiction. Jim Harbaugh, *A 12-Step Approach to the Spiritual Exercises of St. Ignatius* (Kansas City: Sheed & Ward, 1997), 6–7 (SE 15, 179).

of the human situation, and God, who always reached out. I had no doubt that God was inviting me to accompany Patrick on his life's pilgrimage. I saw this as a fruit of my Ignatian Camino: reaching out to those in need.

However, Patrick really struggled with the idea that God could still be with him after the mess he had made of his life. He also felt that any real forgiveness was impossible. I couldn't persuade him otherwise. We did discuss some aspects of Alcoholics Anonymous (AA) recovery that he found helpful, specifically the role of faith in that recovery, though he wasn't a regular member. He was the first person to inadvertently tip me off about how closely linked the 12 Steps of that program are to Ignatian spirituality.[107]

Patrick was born in England, to Irish immigrant parents, and began drinking early as part of what he saw as his Irish cultural heritage. He struggled through school, eventually went to university, and studied business. He was in a very serious car accident at the age of 18, resulting in lasting disability, pain, and limitation, a crushing blow to his dreams of being a professional athlete. Instead, his twenties were spent learning to walk again, recovering the use of his left hand, and beginning a regimen of rehab and exercise that lasts to this day. He worked in teaching and then sales and tried many different jobs, living in a number of different countries before ending up in New Zealand.

In what was the happiest time for him, he was married for seven years before it ended up in a painful divorce. Currently single, facing mid-life issues and many regrets, often weak and sick, and never far from the grip of the demon-booze, he wonders how he ended up like this. He has an impressive desire to overcome, however, and a bloody-minded resolve for things to get better, or at least bearable. He

---

107. A Jesuit helped the founder of Alcoholics Anonymous, Bill Wilson, shape and refine the spirituality of conversion and renewal of life. Robert Fitzgerald, SJ, *The Soul of Sponsorship*, (Center City, MN: Hazelden, 1995); Jim Harbaugh, *A 12-Step Approach to the Spiritual Exercises of St. Ignatius* (Kansas City: Sheed & Ward, 1997).

is a person of faith and prays regularly, though he worries about what God has planned for him, that there may be some harsh judgment in store.

One evening, I was waiting for Patrick to bring me to the parish center, and he was unusually late. I tried phoning him to no avail, and, pressed for time, I had to ask one of my fellow Jesuits to take me. Patrick later apologized profusely for his no-show. He was very remorseful about how he had let me down, especially since it was due to his drinking. He couldn't let it go, though, and I got an insight into the severity of his internal "judge." It seemed that some deeply embedded negative perceptions of faith, such as an image of God as a harsh judge and the punitive understanding of sin and guilt, were holding him prisoner despite my best efforts. If I had learned one thing from my Camino experience, it was not to attribute punishment to God, tempting as it was. To be of help to Patrick, I needed to insulate myself from this negativity, remaining firmly rooted in Christ and in consolation.[108] Fortunately, our relationship recovered from that glitch, and the rest of the course was without incident.

The course concluded well, and the evaluations were very positive. Interestingly, the newly developed approach (less of me, more handing over to God) had proven a lot more effective than my normal one, and I felt invited to a new spiritual freedom to hand over more to God. However, none of this was as significant as what Patrick taught me through our conversations.

Maintaining the commitment to the course and getting to know Patrick had helped me focus my energy on helping others during my recovery in the cast. The time for a follow-up appointment was

---

108. The director has to keep balance and inner freedom in order to be able to help the person involved. Hermann Rodriguez Osorio, "Spiritual Accompaniment during The Spiritual Exercises According to St. Ignatius of Loyola," *Review of Ignatian Spirituality*, No. 108, 73–91.

nearing. I wasn't enthusiastic about that appointment, which was aptly named "Fracture Clinic." I initially felt resistance to attending. However, I knew it was essential and the superficial feelings of resistance shouldn't be prioritized over long-term recuperation. But then I was taken aback when, after five minutes with the doctor, he decided to cut off the cast. "I was just getting used to this," I said, resistant, but the nurse told me it was just for the X-ray and it would probably go back on afterwards. Then she took a very dangerous-looking electric saw to the cast. "It won't cut your skin," she said casually. I found that statement hard to believe as the saw tore into the cast, spitting white plaster dust, my bare flesh just millimeters away. Like a chrysalis casting off its skin, my leg emerged into the light again, raw and pallid. I was sent up to X-ray.

By the time I got back to the Fracture Clinic via elevators and crutches, the doctor already had the X-ray results on the screen. He had read them and come to his surprising diagnosis: "Your leg has healed well; it will be fully healed for the summer, probably, so we'll get you out of the cast and put you in a neoprene brace for the next month or two." I was shocked and delighted. It took some moments for this new reality to sink in as they cleared the scraps of the old cast and introduced a pristine blue brace festooned with Velcro straps. It was like I had been released from prison, set free: Even though I would still have to wear the new brace and move about with crutches for a few weeks, at least sleep would be easier free from the heavy cast. It was a good day, especially as it seemed that I had escaped any long-term injury to the knee.

A week later, a routine appointment with my general practitioner saw me sitting beside a man in the waiting room as I kept my foot elevated on a chair. There is nothing like a physical ailment as an icebreaker between human beings. He asked about my injury and then told me that he had a similar problem. He had been in a motorbike accident and needed fifty-four staples from the ankle up to the knee. He was in a dark place, maybe brought on by the accident and the resulting disability. I thought of Ignatius's convalescence particularly, the deep human drive for health and consolation. However, there is also much hidden suffering in people's lives—I remembered him especially at Mass that night.

At Fracture Clinic, I had been assigned to a physiotherapist in the local health center for rehabilitation work. I felt like a novice again, receiving instruction on a whole new set of skills. The physio stressed the importance of keeping up with the exercises, achieving the target number of repetitions per day, and building up strength over time in order to heal fully. Back at home, wallowing around on the floor, leg muscles weak from lack of use, it was hard to believe that any improvement would happen.[109] It was an exercise of faith. Patrick, who had become a friend, continually impressed on me the need to be faithful to the daily exercises. I think that his timely advice was crucial in the healing process. Though my injury was relatively minor, we had a strong bond and friendship forged in our shared brokenness and vulnerability.

Despite some dark moments of vacilation into and out of desolation, I managed to make progress and gradually added back some small commitments. I once even traveled alone to Dublin on the train for a meeting—no small victory! And on another occasion, I was driven to Cavan, some two hours away, to give a suicide bereavement talk. These journeys were not without their challenges, but they were small steps back to recovery and regaining a sense of normalcy.

---

109. Just as in physical exercise, where the practicing and exercising brings health benefits, the Spiritual Exercises are meditations, prayers, and spiritual practices that through repetition and time bring about integration, freedom, and healing (SE 1).

Six weeks later, the doctor told me that my X-rays were clear. The bone was fully healed. Delighted, I swapped crutches and brace for a lightweight neoprene knee support, a cane, and some new physio exercises. It was a wonderful moment, coming in on crutches and walking out a free man. Unaccustomed to walking, I limped out of the hospital into a dazzling sun. I looked back at the hospital, grateful for the staff, technology, and human support above all. My cousin picked me up and congratulated me warmly. I was still in shock at the transition back to health, gingerly putting weight on the redeemed knee. The leg felt strange, alien, external, and unfettered without the brace. Having been relatively pain-free in the cast for the last few months, the knee now began to throb with the new movement. The bone was healed, but my leg would need to readjust to regular demands of life.

That evening, as a sort of celebration of my regained independence, I walked alone on the country road by my brother's house. It was an epiphany of sights and sounds, the low winter sun, the last withering leaves rustling on the trees, and the quiet dormant landscape. There was the indescribable beauty of walking independently and unhindered through a rural scene. It was a cold, crisp day despite the full sun, but I was relieved and grateful; the world seemed beautiful. My walking was still slow and labored. A lot of the supporting muscles had lost their tone, and I was unused to being on my feet. Thankfully, the cane was helpful on uneven terrain. I knew I was on the right road; joy was in my heart. Winter would be a long one, but I was deeply grateful to my family, the Jesuit community, the physio, and, especially, Patrick. He gave me much needed perspective, a positive approach to recuperation, and the opportunity to keep balanced and in consolation while helping someone.

16

BEATING THE BELFAST BLUES

Winter reigned in Belfast and my recuperation continued, but I felt like I was moving at a snail's pace. Having cancelled or postponed most of my work commitments, I tried to keep some smaller work projects in place, just to have a focus to keep me sane. I was discovering that the most difficult judgment calls were knowing when to push myself, where the limit was, and when to call it a day. If I nursed my newly-healed knee too carefully, I would never leave the house, yet I had to respect some real limitations. My leg was weakened by the time in a cast, and although I could walk unaided, I still opted to use a cane at times. There were yet some months of physio exercises to complete. I felt a certain amount of trial and error was necessary.

In the spirit of putting these new limits to the test, I decided to fulfill a long-standing commitment to give a talk on the Camino de Santiago at the University of Manchester Catholic chaplaincy. It sounded simple enough: sit on a plane for an hour, get picked up by my host, Tim Byron, SJ, do the talk, and rest in between. Of course, these things are never as simple as they seem.

I had already made a trip to Dublin on the train with the crutches. Trying to balance on a moving train had proved challenging, but air travel was in another league. Traveling on a dodgy knee would be physically demanding. The fear of falling was still there, even with the support of a cane. The day before the flight, I realized it would be much easier to travel as a person with a disability, but it was too late to apply for assistance. I wondered if my original reluctance was pride. Was not wanting to admit to a disability preventing me from asking for help?[110] Getting on a plane and managing the various obstacles and hurdles was one thing, but my focus was on overcoming the sense of vulnerability, which could be paralyzing. It was about challenging my fears and proving to myself that I could do it.[111]

My first confrontation with the reality of my situation was at the Belfast airport. Normally, I would have raced through the check-in and boarding process without thinking, but now, even simple things were complicated. Waiting at the security check, shuffling along in a stop-start queue, was draining. Later, trying to get a coffee in the terminal without a free hand was almost impossible. What dominated everything, however, was the unwanted feeling of being underpowered and weak and the scary feeling that I could be easily knocked over. A repeat fall on my knee was my greatest fear. As I reached the plane steps, I hesitated. Fortunately, a member of the cabin crew spotted my dilemma and came forward to assist me in boarding the plane. I was glad to sink into the leather seats on board, though the cramped space meant I couldn't fully stretch out my leg. Safely ensconced for the duration of the flight, I marveled at St. Ignatius travelling on his bad leg in the early 1500s. The leg, shattered by a cannonball and later brutally reset, caused his lifelong limp and much suffering over the course of many arduous journeys. His journeys were genuine pilgrim ones, the vulnerability of being "alone and on foot," full of

110. Pride and particularly self-reliance—that is, having no need of God—are obstacles in the Exercises (SE 142, 322).
111. Not letting fear guide your life is a very concrete spiritual exercise. "Overcoming Temptations of Daily Life," www.loyolapress.com/our-catholic-faith/ignatian-spirituality/finding-god-in-all-things/overcoming-temptations-of-daily-life/.

uncertainty and danger, covering huge distances (up to forty miles a day), while often malnourished and ill.[112] He would have known great pain, suffering, and privations, as well as great illumination, consolation, and joy. I asked for some of his pilgrim spirit now, to find God in my new circumstances, to live trusting in providence, and to depend on God alone.

This abandoning of myself and "handing it over," due to the limitations imposed by injury and my perceived weakness, was the real spiritual challenge. Trusting that there was meaning in whatever little pain and suffering I was experiencing was key to avoiding the feeling that it was empty and random; this was just too devastating a feeling for me. I found inspiration in the image of the suffering Christ: the stripped, beaten, and broken man, abandoned and alone on the cross. His ability to find purpose in his awful experience, even without much immediate consolation, was an invitation to be patient. There were some echoes of his experience present in my vulnerability, my desire for healing, and my hope for a full recovery. I found great comfort in remembering others, including Patrick, who had battled greater odds than I with such courage.

Alighting from the plane in Manchester, I was buoyant at having made it that far. My host, Tim, was warmth personified. A short walk out to the parking lot, and we were driving to the university. Later that evening, after a meal and a tour of the chaplaincy, I shared my Camino de Santiago presentation (the story of my 2011 walk through photos) with a group of students. Sitting, I tightly gripped the cane beside me for security. Normally I would engage with people by moving around the room, but now, it felt like constricted communication, not my best talk. The story seemed to help the attendees, though,

---

112. "Alone and on foot," from the Spanish phrase *solo y a pie*, is closely associated with Ignatius of Loyola, as it captures the key movements and journeys of his life. Brian Grogan, *Alone and on Foot: Ignatius of Loyola* (Dublin: Veritas, 2008).

providing something for that human desire for healing. And I was thankful for their thoughtful questions. Reflecting afterwards, however, I felt there was learning for me in finding a new presentation format, having the story speak for itself in photographs, which appeared to be more powerful.

The next day, on the noisy propeller plane back home to Belfast, I was somewhat drained. Head resting on the window, I reflected again that I had a whole new understanding of St. Ignatius's story. His personal writings and dictated autobiography seemed to play down his experience of disability, as if it were secondary to his conversion, but my hunch was that it was pivotal. Having had one leg shattered and the other badly damaged in Pamplona in 1521, he was forced to abandon his former courtier way of life and became a bedbound invalid for many months. The enforced immobility brought about his daydreaming and reflection. He accidentally uncovered God's stirrings in his interior, which was the catalyst for his subsequent transformation.

A Jesuit psychoanalyst attributes his conversion to the profound physical consequences of the bodily wounds: the sense of defeat, his enforced passivity, immobility, and dependence on others.[113] The traumatic blow to his body image, the shattering of his physically attractive, "powerful knight" ego ideal, produced enormous internal psychic forces, a painful reforming. This was the genesis of his reinventing himself as a poor pilgrim, rejecting vanity, superficiality, and "worldliness." Ignatius was now "in the service of a heavenly king," ever the knight in search of a great cause. Ignatius had switched allegiance and affection to Christ, the spiritual king. The physical wound had echoed through all the levels of his psyche, remodeling the

---

113. Ignatius's ordeals of body and spirit during his career as a soldier drove the psychic and psychodynamic inner processes that led him to change his life in ways that would transform him into a saint. W. W. Meissner, *Ignatius of Loyola: The Psychology of a Saint* (New Haven, CT: Yale University, 1992), 366.

old person and reshaping him entirely. The question again arose of the meaning in my physical suffering and the apparent "disaster" as to what change God was inviting me into. The great Ignatian phrase of "finding God in all things" was sorely tested in the forge of disability, a negative experience. What was this deeper process that was playing itself out? Exiting the airport, I wondered if there was enlightenment or new direction for me.

Soon after my trip to Manchester, I began meeting people again for spiritual direction or pastoral counseling. Given the restriction on my mobility, listening to people, giving some feedback, and being attentive were all within my abilities. Working with those bereaved by suicide especially had become more significant. I had written and spoken widely on the theme.[114] With my own personal experience, it was about being there for others going through a similar process and providing a safe place for people to talk. One of those recently widowed was Laura, whose husband I had known through the parish. We had met a number of times, and those had been deeply painful and harrowing sessions.

Laura had been through the mill of grief and loss, surviving as a single mom, but she was beginning to come out the other side. Directly after her husband's death was a period of extreme darkness where she felt abandoned, rejected, alone, and confused. In particular, she felt devoid of any sense of God, which was particularly disturbing for her. Gradually she had opened, courageously talked about her husband, and grieved deeply and openly at times. Making memories from photos had helped; she walked and exercised a lot and decided to train in a new career. It was in her asking the question "Why?" (blaming God for what had happened) that she was led to a sense of God's absence, although this gradually dissolved over time as she saw God as less responsible for it. She saw love and compassion in the people around

---

114. A booklet in the Messenger series: Brendan McManus, SJ, *Surviving Suicide Bereavement: Finding Life after Death* (Dublin: Messenger Publications, 2016).

her, realizing that this was God's work. Her deep faith, will to survive, and coping skills were impressive. She really lived the grief process deeply and with heartfelt emotion.

The important thing was for me to listen; she knew she had a sympathetic ear from someone who had "been there." Mostly, I felt a great compassion and sacredness at witnessing her grief, although later I did wonder at how I was able to put my own pain to one side so easily.

As winter progressed, life continued to improve. With religious completion of my physio exercises, my knee gradually felt better, and my confidence in it grew. My spiritual recovery back from the desolation I had felt in the cast was progressing in stride with my physical rehabilitation. That is, until one overcast evening when it was abruptly halted by a short text message from another priest: "Watch RTE Investigates program tonight."[115] The TV listings didn't indicate a specific topic, but I had an ominous premonition that this would be serious. I was worried about what would be revealed.

The program that night made a series of allegations about mismanagement and financial irregularities within the charity that I was heavily involved with in my suicide bereavement work. I had given the proceeds of my book to the charity and subsequently been a spokesperson for them. It was still unclear what the final outcome would be for the charity, but the fallout for me was clear. I would have to cut ties. With my recent Camino ending in failure, now this?! It was tempting to think that everything was falling apart. It was the undermining of yet another pillar in my vocation that I thought was unshakeable.

I felt I had been left stranded on a beach of fading memories: a failed Camino, a wounded pilgrim, difficulty in prayer, and now the charity going under. My immediate reaction was resentment toward

---

115. RTE is the Irish National TV broadcaster, and *RTE Investigates* is an investigative journalism program.

God, feeling he could have made things easier for me, but I knew I had to get some perspective and not react out of the raw emotion.[116] I had to place my small worries into context and take a longer view. I was putting all these things together as one stream of negative experiences, but they were different things. The charity collapsing was unrelated to any of the other circumstantial events in my life. The Ignatian Camino walk had ended in injury, but it had been nothing serious or permanent. My expectations for that walk had been too high due to my previous experience, but I could not live in the past. Spiritually, I could now see that I had gotten a little bit lax and complacent, drifting somewhat, and getting a bit carried away with the 2011 Camino afterglow.[117]

The inflated expectations for the Ignatian Camino, my desire for the same feeling I had gotten from my 2011 Camino de Santiago, and my stubbornness in letting go of those attachments had made accepting the reality of my injury difficult. Something had to bring me down to earth, quite exactly what the fall had done. This was not the end of the story, however. I now found myself in a place of transition, on another journey of recovery, or purification, where I could not see ahead too clearly. The physical recovery from injury was relatively straightforward, but it was the spiritual and emotional challenges that complicated things, especially overcoming my negativity and passivity. I needed to regain my confidence in myself and God. It felt like my daily life had become the new Camino, and I was a pilgrim in process, hobbling and shuffling along a dark road. The challenges were inner ones, a dark interior landscape of emotions, desires, and expectations, which made the road difficult to navigate.

---

116. Affective maturity or "ordering emotions" is the ability to feel and to experience emotions but to work with them and not be at their mercy (SE 21).
117. After a great experience or spiritual high, there is often an "afterglow" or hankering back where you continue to live on the memory of previous experience; Ignatius warns that this can be deceptive (SE 336).

What had kept me going was the Ignatian insight that integration of the recent Camino wasn't about transient feelings but rather a deeper sense of awareness of God's presence. In this respect, other people's stories helped me greatly. I kept walking on in trust through this "dark night" of recuperation, believing in an imminent dawn. Patience, perseverance, and hope were my companions in the absence of positive consolation.

Ignatius of Loyola has a number of rules for discernment specifically related to handling desolation. He also identifies some possible causes for it. He gives three principal reasons for desolation: through our own fault (e.g., laziness), by taking consolation for granted (as a right, not a gift), and as a way for God to reveal to us the true source of consolation.[118] The last two really spoke to me: God's removal of consolation was to purify and teach some important insights about vigilance and taking things for granted. It was true that after the 2011 Camino, I had gotten used to living in consolation, as if I had a right to it, which had led to a shock at its absence. Maybe I had gotten too complacent, or had been lax in my prayer, and had forgotten how hard won the insights from the Camino de Santiago had been. The rules for discernment cautioned about seeking the solace and rewards of God's love without wanting to live through the process or journey of getting there. Maybe that journey was the one that I was currently engaged in, trying to remain faithful and hang on in the midst of pain and doubt. Maybe there was some hidden lesson in this recent frustrating, and apparently empty, Camino experience.

In addition, Ignatius also outlined a series of rules for combating desolation, which are equally practical and useful. He recommends shoring up inner defenses and not making any major decisions or changes in course.[119] The image he uses is that of a fortress under

---

118. Michael Ivens, *Understanding the Spiritual Exercises* (Leominster, England: Gracewing, 1998); (SE 221–23, 317–27).

attack by a crafty enemy who exploits the weak points or design flaws to gain entry and overthrow the castle.[120] Successful defense means knowing and fortifying one's weak points, understanding that the wily enemy comes in the back door and in disguise. My weakness here had been the attachment to the past experience of God on the Camino de Santiago, and when I wasn't feeling the warmth of God's love as I had on that Camino, the temptation was to think God had left me. The enemy was attacking these vulnerable points of hope and faith, because these fundamental beliefs were the key to undermining the whole architecture of my faith. Thanks to Ignatius, I had some understanding of how I was being deceived. Another rule stated that I possessed sufficient love and grace to carry on being faithful, even though I felt abandoned and couldn't sense God's presence directly. More than anything else, this really seemed to capture the paradox of where I found myself: bereft of any consoling feelings, washed up by a tide of negativity, and having to trust that God was still in this experience of blind faith.

The remainder of winter was long, and the healing was very slow. Life revolved around physiotherapy, spiritual direction, and actively working against desolation. I was reminded of Patrick, my driver in my time of need, who had advised me to do all the exercises religiously. Physio meant having to tolerate increased pain and discomfort through the daily exercises in the short term, in the belief that things would get better in the long term. The same was true for my spiritual life: I had to keep a regular rhythm of prayer, receiving

---

119. Ignatius recommends not making any significant changes; rather, change things in ourselves that would help the situation, such as prayer, meditation, and penance; remain faithful and develop patience (SE 318–21); resist the aggressive or seductive tactics of the bad spirit by holding one's ground, shoring up defenses, and getting advice (SE 325–27).

120. I recently wrote an article on this metaphor. www.jesuit.ie/blog/brendan-mcmanus/spiritual-defence-and-game-of-thrones/

the Eucharist, and reflection in the current absence of consolation or pleasant feelings. Keeping faithful to this routine, doing the physical and spiritual exercises, would see me through. As the days grew longer and the hope of the inevitable return of spring reentered my mind, I knew consolation would come eventually.

17

THE POPE AND I

It had been a challenging year. By summer, I was itching to get into the mountains and test my newly rehabilitated knee. The perfect opportunity arose in the form of a Jesuit group of young adults going to World Youth Day (WYD) in Poland, the international summer event for young Catholics presided over by Pope Francis himself. Prior to this huge event of several million young people, there was a smaller Jesuit preparatory event called MAGIS.[121] This was the Ignatian spiritual preparation for WYD and gave young people tools for prayer, faith sharing, and worship. There was a group of nineteen young people and five leaders going, and I signed up to be one of the support leaders. A key part of this eighteen-day experience would be a variety of group activities in and around Poland. I signed up for a five-day walking pilgrimage in the Snieznik Mountains, a mountain range in the Eastern Sudetes, on the border with the Czech Republic. On Google Earth, I digitally flew through its canyons, pine valleys, and fault lines. It was the ideal place to test my hiking abilities—a step up from the Irish mountains. I was hungry to get back to the wild and see if I was restored to my pre-fall capabilities.

---

121. *Magis* is a Latin word used by Ignatius, often translated as "more" but meaning "deeper" in the sense of a reflective moment to become aware of where God is leading and make decisions accordingly. What is Magis, www.magis2016.org.

Early one Friday morning in July, our group met in Dublin Airport's Terminal 2 for our flight to Poland. Arriving in Warsaw, we stretched our legs briefly before being whisked off by our contact in a bus to the city of Lodz, in the center of Poland. A university campus was the venue for this first part of the MAGIS program. Everything was well organized, and in no time we were presented with our identity badges, MAGIS hoodies, and T-shirts. The accommodations were in simple, shared student dorm rooms and shared facilities, which reminded me of a Camino-style pilgrimage.

It wasn't long before the PA system was cranked up, and we were led by two presenters in praise and worship songs that featured dance moves. As befitting a youth event, it was high energy, high volume, and featured lots of flag waving, dancing, handclapping, and running around. All the events, from morning to evening prayer, Mass, and worship, were held in an outdoor all-weather field. Fortunately, the weather cooperated. The head of the Jesuits worldwide, Fr. Adolfo Nicolas, the eighty-year-old Superior General of the Jesuits, addressed us via video link on the importance of the placements—testing experiences similar to those in Jesuit formation—that we would undertake over the next few days. I felt a stab of fear, realizing for the first time that the pilgrimage would certainly be demanding. I couldn't help but entertain the image of me limping alone through the woods.

A central part of the MAGIS program, the placements, had young people broken up into small groups of around twenty to thirty and sent off to a range of locations in Poland and neighboring countries. The activities included walking, dance, art, theatre, service, and social placements. The key Ignatian elements common to all groups were daily prayer, periods of silence/reflection, the daily Examen (review of the day), and the MAGIS circle (faith sharing in a group). A nervous thrill ran through me, hearing my name read out as part of the walking pilgrimage group. This time I was going as a participant, in a support role, and not as a leader as I normally would. With my rehabilitated knee largely untested, there were a lot of unknowns. However, I was excited and as worked up as the young people, whose enthusiasm was infectious. Sitting on the ground with other group members from Portugal, Belgium, Slovakia, Holland, and Ireland, we introduced ourselves individually, and then our Polish leaders, Magda and Wojciech, SJ, briefed us on the road that lay ahead.

After a whole day's bus journey through striking meadows, forests, and endless farmland, we were dropped at the edge of a huge pine forest as evening fell. An expectant silence enveloped us as we padded up a short laneway through stands of pines and farm buildings. Our pilgrim existence had begun. After a night in a simple hostel that smelled strongly of pine, we began walking in the massif that is the Snieznik Mountains. My first few steps were charged with excitement and nerves in equal measure. Our Polish guides had warned us that the first day would be very tough and mainly uphill; it was to be a challenging morning. Out of condition, I labored at the back of the group, largely young and bright twenty-year-olds able to walk and talk simultaneously. I knew that it would take me a few days just to get into the rhythm and that I would need patience. I practiced looking for gratitude in toiling up huge hills, experiencing the regular downpours, sharing rooms with others, and living in close quarters (we were to spend one night in tents).[122] I kept hearing the persistent inner voice say *You are getting too old for this* but knew enough to disregard it.

The sober beauty of the Polish forest, endless pines, and striking silences (we walked in silence praying for an hour a day) was our stable diet. Rustic villages, simple agriculture, and old tractors were the only signs of life. The second day was the most testing for me, and

---

122. Seeking to cultivate an "attitude of gratitude" that transforms an experience (SE 32–43).

realizing my limits as evening approached, I accepted a ride in the support car. If I had learned anything from my Ignatian Camino, it was about reading the body and not pushing myself too far. Rather, the important thing was to be on the journey, sharing in the experience, and trying to see things as God sees them. Gradually the rhythm of feet, soundless pine needles, and a canopy of trees began to work its magic. We were living from a deeper place: connected to ourselves, each other, and God. The fluidity of walking in a group meant that I got to speak with each person individually, and I was greatly heartened by these young people's stories. I recognized a familiar echo of tough moments and sorrow, prayer that had helped them through difficult circumstances; and a God of proximity and compassion. Like the burnt section of forest we passed at one stage, storms and apparent devastation were not the end but an opening for new growth of inner freedom, peace, and joy. I saw my Camino injury in this same light. Slowly the walk began to bring about its transforming spell, rooting us in our experience, integrating the group, and opening possibilities. I felt some new hope emerge; the dark cloud was shifting, and my life was being restored and healed.

On the third day, we ascended a long, craggy ridge, eventually emerging from the fog of toil and struggle to a rocky viewpoint. The panoramic view had us stop and stare at the wonder of nature. Interlocking hills and wispy clouds stretched off into the distance, an undulating wilderness. That night was a high point, a rocky mountain-top hostel with a dizzying view of rich farmland spread out below. We were irresistibly drawn to the sunset viewpoint, a magnificent luminosity of transcendental beauty. The owner invited us to come in from the outside terrace at dusk and showed us into a vault-like, stone-walled room with two guitars. This evening turned into a lovely musical gathering, helping us get over language barriers and cultural differences. I even picked up the guitar again after a long break, my fingers and voice raw from lack of practice. It was an experience of great joy, being part of this exuberance and expression, even more so because I knew that I had walked through adversity to be here. I even did my party piece, an impersonation of Bono of U2 singing the song "One," complete with sunglasses. With this truly great group of supportive young people, I felt like a pilgrim again. This company, in that place in the clouds, revealed the face of God in harmony, transformation, and equality. I was in heaven on earth.

I was where God wanted me to be. I felt young again, freed from the expectations and false chains of age. It was energizing to get back on the road after a long absence, to breathe in the fresh air, to feel the sun and wind on my face, and to walk free of injury. It was also a gift to be a listening ear for the young people and to work as part of the team of leaders, though now in a supporting role. I reflected that one of the hardest things about being sick or injured is the blow it deals to the spirit. Rehabilitation is not just a physical process, it's the whole coming back to life of all the rusty bits of ourselves. We need rehab and healing for all those different dimensions of ourselves: body, mind, and spirit.

On the last night of the pilgrimage, I unexpectedly had to share a room with more than thirty others and sleep on the floor. I got little to no sleep due to the final party celebrations and had to do without a morning shower. However, I was able to adjust, go with it, and surprisingly enjoyed it. I felt that God was gently teaching me more lessons and asking me to relinquish control.[123] In fact it was liberating to realize all the preconditions and expectations that can dampen our daily experience and sever our connection with real joy, joy from the

---

123. Ignatian freedom is about freely accepting any conditions or circumstances as gifts, without being limited by preconceptions or expectations, in order to find the newness of God in situations. Trying to maintain control is the opposite, a common human "disordered attachment" where the ego seeks to control and "order" outcomes (SE 21).

Gospel. God's call seemed to be one of simplicity, connection, and trust, with a little bit of living on the edge!

Then, all at once the Jesuit program was over, and we were on a bus for Krakow and the second part of our pilgrimage: World Youth Day (WYD) with Pope Francis. This was a whole other dynamic, though. We moved from the intimacy of MAGIS to the massiveness of WYD, where everything was multiplied by a factor of thousands. It was like going from a pond to the sea. We arrived at a parish in the Grzegorzecka district of Krakow, lucky enough to be twenty minutes from the city center. Some other groups would have huge commutes, over an hour or two away. Our Irish youth group was based in a school gym, and as a priest, I was sharing with a group of seven other priests on bunk beds in the parish rectory. It took awhile for us to get registered, and it seemed that every half hour another group of Irish pilgrims from some diocese would arrive and camp outside the doorway.

The WYD schedule includes bishops leading catechesis in the mornings to different language groups, afternoon workshops, and seminars around the city, and different liturgies with Pope Francis in the evening. Before coming, I had volunteered at one of the three Jesuit MAGIS Cafés promoting the Jesuits and all things Ignatian around Krakow. I was working in the smallest MAGIS Café, an escape for pilgrims in a quiet courtyard in the Jesuit curia building just off the main square. It was designed as a place of relaxation and reflection amid a very noisy and extroverted WYD event. Every morning, I would leave the Irish group to their catechesis and make my way into the walled city for work, welcoming pilgrims and trying to help those needing to talk. As a spiritual director, this was right up my street.

That evening, seeing Pope Francis (a dot in the distance) was a great moment where the head of the Catholic Church was present to us in the muddy reality of the "field," a huge grassy park packed with almost a million young pilgrims. The pope's address about not living a "halfway" Christianity but giving generously struck a chord with me in terms of a practical spirituality that engages the world and seeks to help people. I had a new insight about being a pilgrim in everyday life as much as being out walking on a trail. This was bringing pilgrim attitudes of seeking God and responding well to different situations into daily living. Every day was a new journey; it was an openness to the spirit working in ordinary things in everyday life. The Camino was something that could be lived daily. Life was the great pilgrim challenge, and relationships were both the challenge and the joy. Reflecting on Mary's grace, I saw that it was about being humble and receptive, in order to allow great things to happen through us. Imitating Christ was everything; he was the ultimate pilgrim.

Everything built up to our last night on WYD: a prayer vigil with the pope, sleeping under the stars, and then the final Sunday Mass under an open sky. The ten-mile walk out to the *Campus Misericordiae* or "field of mercy" was difficult in the heat, and we had to stop frequently to rest and drink fluids. The site itself with rusting machinery, gravel roads, and small lakes was actually an abandoned quarry. As it was a totally outdoor event, it involved camping in a field, tightly packed beside others, a challenging setting, though youthful enthusiasm overcame all obstacles.

The vigil with the pope was one of the most moving moments of the whole event as dusk fell and emotions were intensified. I shared earphones with an Irish woman to hear Rand Mittri, a twenty-six-year-old Syrian woman talk about the destruction of Aleppo. A visibly moved Pope Francis called on youth not to be "couch potatoes" but to be "alert and searching, trying to respond to God's dream and to all the restlessness present in the human heart," underlining that they weren't here to "vegetate, to take it easy" but to "leave a mark."[124]

Finally, the lighting of personal candles transformed the field into a sea of lights, reflecting the hope and individual mission for each person. Kneeling in that field, holding my candle, and my *Yes* connected in prayer to the pope and the million others present, I understood *vigil* anew in terms of being given a second chance, wakefulness, and openness to the world.

Waking up the next morning was a challenge. Thirsty and unshaven, I blinked in the bright sun at the sea of bodies in all directions. With another Irish priest, Alan, we went off early to concelebrate the Mass with the pope, queuing for our white WYD vestments. We found a spot to sit on the saturated, marshy ground, still far from the main altar. At one stage, Pope Francis in the popemobile passed within a few hundred yards of us waving. Excitedly, we waved back. Soon the saturated soil turned to mud and one of my enduring images of the Mass was devout priests robed in white, trying to shield themselves from the sun, with mud staining their shoes and vestments. It was a symbol for all of us of our pilgrim nature, our "feet of clay," and the divine redemption of our earthly nature.

Jorge Mario Bergoglio, SJ, who would become Pope Francis, was born in 1936 in Buenos Aires, Argentina. His surname reveals his Italian roots; his father emigrated from Italy in 1929, fleeing the Mussolini regime. Bergoglio was the oldest of five children and always had wide interests including soccer, reading, and dancing the tango. At the age of twenty, he nearly died from pneumonia; it resulted in cysts that necessitated the removal of part of his right lung, a condition that affects him to this day and affected his

---

124. Pope Francis, Prayer Vigil with the Young People, World Youth Day, Krakow, 30 July 2016. www.vatican.va/content/francesco/en/speeches/2016/july/documents/papa-francesco_20160730_polonia-veglia-giovani.html.

Jesuit training. He worked as a chemical technician, also as a janitor, and a bar doorman for a while. Despite his mother's urgings to be a doctor, Bergoglio felt a call to the priesthood.

Like St. Ignatius, the impaired Bergoglio gave himself fully to the formation process, to prayer and discernment. Distinguishing himself as a leader, in 1973, at the age of just thirty-six, he was made Provincial, the head of all Jesuits in Argentina and neighboring Uruguay. This coincided with Argentina's military coup and the so-called "dirty war" that threatened "leftist" Jesuits and caused huge divisions in the Province. Bergoglio later acknowledged that his inexperience and autocratic style didn't help, as he polarized opinion in the Jesuit Province, and after fifteen years he was exiled, first to Germany and then to Córdoba, Argentina, a far-flung outpost where he was to experience, in his own words, "a time of great interior crisis." This time of prayer and purification, or "dark night," was to bring about profound change in the future pope in terms of humility, patience, and compassion. Bergoglio, in an article from that time, cites the cross and the Passion of Jesus as where the divinity appears to be hidden during a trial of great suffering.

In 1992, he was rescued from obscurity, picked as auxiliary bishop for Buenos Aires, and then archbishop in 1998. Bergoglio was elevated to cardinal in 2001. He was elected Pope in 2013, a surprise to many, becoming the first-ever Jesuit pope. Arguably, the painful lessons he learned through his "dark night" are instrumental in his mission of transforming the Catholic Church: moving its focus toward the importance of listening, collegiality, genuine humility, the option for the poor, and praxis approach to theology.

Ironically, my walk back alone to our host parish in Krakow was the most difficult moment: the hot tar, humidity, and thirst contributed to a pounding headache, and I didn't feel well. I could really relate to the words of Psalm 63: "My soul thirsts for you; my flesh faints for you, as in a dry and weary land where there is no water." Now I had a new understanding of these words as I walked in this 86-degree heat, impossible humidity, and thunderstorms looming. The crowds of people slowed to a snail's pace; ominous thunderstorms, intermittent downpours, and humidity all worked to intensify the thirst. I was overwhelmed with a sense of claustrophobia on the never-ending, boiling, hard road. Like a madman, I was drinking everything I could get my hands on; at one stage I went into a bodega and drank a liter of sports drink straight down. Once back, I collapsed into my camp bed and tried to get cool and rehydrate, unaware that I was suffering symptoms of heat stroke. I was too sick to make the Irish coach leaving for Warsaw that evening, where they would stay overnight in order to catch an early flight home the following day. I had no choice but to text the leader, Niall, my apologies. Wearily I resigned myself to an uneasy sleep, the drama of the day written into my worn and fatigued body.

After a few hours' sleep, I woke up at midnight feeling decidedly better. Some rehydration salts given to me by another priest had a marked effect on my well-being. In what became my eleventh-hour deliverance, I met one of the Polish volunteers on duty, and he brought me to an early train for Warsaw, which would get me to the airport just in time to rejoin the group for the flight home. In the train carriage, I sat opposite a Polish family, and the father, Jacek, enthusiastically engaged me about WYD and photography, his passion. Graciously, he offered me a takeaway coffee from the bar, but the lid wasn't on properly, and he spilt the coffee all over me. Though initially I reacted with anger, the giggles from the daughter and mother were intoxicating. All I could do then was laugh with them. It was a kind of anointing (the coffee had spilt mostly on my knee!). The God of Surprises at work once more, bringing me back down to earth, and blessing me.[125] Several hours later I was home in Belfast, happier than ever to see my own bed.

It struck me that those eighteen days in Poland were every much a pilgrimage as was the Camino, maybe even more so. I felt it was a falling in love with life again, with pilgrimage, and with the infectious enthusiasm of young people. I felt the same grace I had received from the 2011 Camino, in a new setting: a renewal of energies and faith. It was almost exactly a year since I had fallen and busted my knee in Spain. I felt I could close that chapter of convalescence and healing. Despite everything, I was amazingly restored to full health and could get on with life and my commitments. I was thinking about getting back into my work in suicide bereavement and mental health, and especially my new role in training clergy. I was in a better place to talk about them. However, I was also conscious of some underlying reluctance in me to taking up this burden once again.

125. Gerard W. Hughes, *God of Surprises* (London: Darton, Longman & Todd, 1986).

18

WINTER'S END

The rush of energy and enthusiasm of Poland soon faded during September, and life gravitated back to normal. With mixed feelings, I hung up my boots and my pilgrim attire, conscious of the ongoing reflection process that was still playing itself out. Having unpacked and stowed my sleeping bag and camping gear, I settled into my normal work routine in Belfast. I stepped back into the rhythm of travel and talks, and I was quickly in the thick of that work. Luckily, a providentially late onset of autumn was softening the blow of cold weather.

In what was to be a defining moment, late October saw me presenting a training workshop in Enniskillen to clergy and key workers on "Suicide Prevention and Mental Health." My opening words were: "Surviving suicide bereavement is a lot more complicated than you think. I know because I have been there." Part of my final assessment as a trainer, what was to have been the culmination of my training and the integration of insights from suicide bereavement work, was not evident that day, however. Although I had essentially given the same talk for over two years, this time I labored and struggled, in part because I was feeling under the weather with a flu, but even more so, I struggled emotionally. Using personal anecdotes and sharing about my bereavement experience was a powerful part of my delivery and normally felt very rewarding and fruitful. This time, however, it felt painful and disturbing, like opening an old wound. While debriefing afterwards with the psychologist-trainer, Conor, I confessed my concern. In contrast, he hadn't noticed this aspect and thought the presentation was great! Outside, the languid Erne River flashed the afternoon sun off the sixteenth-century castle but failed to lift my spirits. On the long road to Belfast, I sank into a gloomy low and arrived as darkness fell. My mind was filled with questioning thoughts: *How could I be feeling this way doing something I normally loved? Why was my spirit so agitated?*

Being ill for a short while after my talk gave me time and space to reflect on my negative feelings from it. The REM song, "Everybody Hurts," had a special resonance for me during this time. The unexpected negativity surrounding this experience initially made me want to pass over it, dismiss it, forget all about it. Having tried that, I knew that approach solved nothing. I had to let the slow process of reflection reveal its message to me over time. I would have to stay with the difficult feelings. As always, it was a paradoxical feeling: I felt unease tinged with an edge of promise.[126] Within the Ignatian world, every experience is significant, and God is present in it all, somewhere, communicating and inviting us to find meaning. This can be difficult to accept when you are at a low point or when, like me, you are resistant to looking into things too closely for fear of what you might find. Reflection is the tool that allows us to slow down, look more closely, clear out the dross, and see what substance is contained within.

I knew that the clues were in the experience itself. I just needed to pay attention to it and pray with it in order to reveal its secrets. It is more akin to contemplating a scene that slowly reveals its beauty than attacking a problem like a dog, breaking a bone open to get to the marrow. Staying with it and focused is key to discovery. This was

---

126. Desolation is double edged in that it is an unpleasant wake-up call but also a way back to God (SE 317).

easier said than done. The workshop had a heavy negative emotional hue for me. When I compared it to other workshops I had given, it lacked the passion and consoling sense of satisfaction afterwards. Why was this experience so different? What had changed? It was true that I had been laboring under a flu and this seemingly accounted for the discrepancy, but was there something else?

Some weeks went by before I took some time alone in my November-darkened room with a notebook and a determination to face into this discernment process. I looked at all the different possibilities and implications: *Was this just a temporary blip because I was ill at the time?* In that case, the important thing was that I made it through the assessment (the end justifies the means). Or, as the workshop had gone well, I thought, *Was it just another lesson not to overdo things while feeling ill?* Maybe it was just a matter of changing my approach for a new audience (i.e., for clergy or community leaders), as they were not actually the suicide bereaved, a necessary change of style and delivery. What struck me most forcibly was that I was feeling the normally hidden cost and the emotional weight of this suicide work. It was an awareness that was difficult to square with my passion for this work and my great commitment to it. Gradually, as I reviewed my thoughts, I became aware of how, over the last two years, I had been prioritizing the bereavement work above all else. The recent pilgrimage in Poland had given me a critical distance and perspective that allowed me fresh insights: *Had such important work and outreach to the grieving become "untouchable"? Was I so personally invested in it that I wasn't discerning about it or "free" (detached, in an Ignatian sense) about it?*

A weekend in late November doing a supply run in Newcastle, County Down, gave me the chance to breathe some sea air. There, I walked the great pebble beach in the bitter cold mornings and beheld the Mourne Mountains standing sentry behind the bay. Exploring the area further, I came upon St. John's Point, the northernmost end of Dundrum Bay. When I saw the lighthouse and the rocky point extending into the sea, I was immediately reminded of Finisterre in Spain. The memory of that enormous journey on the Camino in 2011 and the healing I had received was written into my soul. My tears in Finisterre had been mingled with the earth there. Now I could feel the emotion rising, thinking about it. As I sat on the rough jetty, I prayed in thanks for that time. Suddenly, the words of Isaiah came to me:

> Remember not the former things, nor consider the things of old. Behold, I am doing a new thing; now it springs forth, do you not perceive it?[127]

I had to accept that something was stirring, and I was resisting it. I had an image of my experience in Finisterre in 2011 like a boat lashed to its moorings, constricted and immobile, yet tossed by the waves. I felt the weight of being chained to something I held dear that was also dragging me down. It was a heartrending challenge; my Ignatian Camino experience had opened a new perspective on my beloved bereavement work, and I found myself reluctant to face what this would mean. I wasn't ready to cast off the moorings yet, but I realized there was some attachment or inner tie that stopped me from being free.[128]

December revealed the issue. It was far from being resolved and continued to bubble away on the edge of my consciousness. Even as I busied myself with other activities and work, some hidden, inexorable process had been set in motion. This was interesting as it revealed a disproportionate commitment that was clearly due to emotional

---

127. Isaiah 43:18–19
128. Achieving genuine freedom is about making healthy and reasoned (discerned) decisions about what God wants of us, facing our fears, and especially acting against unhealthy attachments (SE 149–55).

factors: my identification with the bereaved, the desire to help others, and playing down the real personal and emotional costs.[129] I couldn't continue with my energies dispersed over so many fronts. I would have to prioritize, for my own sake and for the quality of my work. This was sobering, yet useful, and I attempted to rate my current priorities in a list from most to least important. Then, I tried to draw a line in the list. Above the line were those commitments that were manageable, and below, those that I needed to look at more closely. The suicide bereavement work would feature in the top half, for sure, and fixedly, I thought, *What else could I drop instead?* Even though it seemed to me that there was some attachment or "unfreedom" operating here, I wasn't ready to face it yet.

A tiring trip to Donegal in driving rain made me aware of my real limits. *I must do something about this*, I resolved. It was only subsequently, when I went to see my spiritual director, that I managed to get some perspective. My director helped me see that being too attached emotionally might not be a good thing. I needed to let an air of freedom blow rather than keep clinging on tightly. I began to have a series of disturbing dreams. In one of them I was trying to help a young girl but failed to see her needs clearly. I began to see that I was blind to some ideas and priorities and that I was resisting positive change. I had been caught up in idealism and illusion. In discernment terms, I was trapped in the pride and prestige of overidentifying with one thing.[130] What was so subtle about it was that it canonized my own woundedness in relation to suicide but kept me a

---

129. This is called a "disordered" or unhealthy attachment. Vinita Hampton Wright, "What Is an Unhealthy Attachment?" www.ignatianspirituality.com/what-is-an-unhealthy-attachment/.

130. To be really free and indifferent to things means being able to hold them lightly, to let them go if needed so that we can remain focused on what God wants and not what we want. Sometimes we make deals with God to hold onto what we want (SE 149–57).

prisoner there, continually reopening this old wound and not allow-ing it to heal. While this often does work for some people and had been really worthwhile for me for three years, I felt it wasn't work-ing for me anymore. I remembered again Ignatius's enlightenment in Manresa: things that seem to be good on the surface may be bringing us in a bad direction. Slowly, I recognized that this was not what God was calling me to, the emotionally draining nature of this work, and that this would continue to be an issue into the future. Something had to give. The emotional cost was evident, but *how would I let go of something I had worked so hard at or step back from an area I had invested myself in so deeply?* Ruefully, I sensed the jigsaw pieces begin to click into place.

As the winter solstice and Christmas approached, I was clear that the unease following the clergy conference in Enniskillen had been a sign and a wakeup call to action. I committed to withdrawing from my work in suicide bereavement and within a few weeks had made the necessary arrangements. There was, however, a period of doubt afterwards: *Have I done the right thing? Did I make a mistake?* I knew I wouldn't see the benefits of it immediately, but only after some time.

The year started into January, and things did improve, though slowly and incrementally. It was like a weight was being slowly lifted off my shoulders. I missed the old sense of purpose and meaning, for sure, but I was surprised at how much relief I felt not to be revisiting the theme of suicide. I suspected that this unease had been present for some time previously and that the fall on the Ignatian Camino, the subsequent rehabilitation, and the recent experience of consola-tion in Poland had led me to this breakthrough. I felt like scales were coming off my eyes, just like St. Paul's, in realizing my previous blind-ness. Real freedom, like a well in the desert, began to slowly work its magic. Though I hadn't noticed the aridity creeping in over time, the flowering of the oasis was breathtaking. For the first time in a long while, I had time and energy for work, for people, and for prayer. I think my posture and walking improved too, free from injury, stress, or excess weight. I especially found comfort in Psalm 42: "As a deer longs for flowing streams, so my soul longs for you, O God" because it contrasted with the terrible drought I'd felt for the previous year of recovery with longing for God's presence and arrival.

I had made it through the darkness of another northern winter into spring. With the emergence of new life outside in nature, I began to see my Ignatian Camino experience in a new light. Far from a disaster, it was actually a profound encounter with God, playing itself out slowly over time and revealing its riches through careful reflection. I did notice one significant difference compared with my previous ecstatic 2011 Camino experience. Six years before, I had been deeply touched, experienced healing, and floated on a cloud for a number of years afterward. This time, the catharsis was much more sobering and down-to-earth, more realistic, and grounded, solemn. It was more like a slow burn than a great explosion. Now I felt more balanced, realistic, and measured. This fit with Ignatius's sense of genuine consolation, how it operates in real-life settings, and how the emphasis should be on "the God of consolations rather than on the consolation of God."[131] As a school teacher instructs a child, I was being taught, again, that learning never stops. Falling on the Ignatian Camino was filled with learning, invitations to let go of control and experience a new freedom with God's help.

Then it came to me: The clergy workshop and its aftermath was a blessing as it led to this great liberation, just like falling on the Camino had been a great blessing too. I had come to the realization of the true cost of bereavement work and that I needed to move on from it. I could finally see the whole process clearly. Taking the

---

131. When we start to seek consolation or the good feeling for its own sake, it becomes an attachment itself and freedom is lost (SE 316).

long view, the challenges of pain, crutches, restricted movement, and rehabilitation were essential to the insights and wisdom gained from the experience. Through that trial, God had taught me about taking the time needed for the reflective process, being more receptive than active (handing over to God), being open to the way that God works through situations and people, and learning new skills of discernment (what is the genuine good?). The whole "fall" experience had been about trusting God more, not getting carried away with my own projects, and discerning more carefully. Realizing I needed to withdraw from suicide bereavement was the fruit of the slow work of awareness, sifting feelings, and reflection that had begun on the Camino and subsequent recuperation from my injury. The discernment process had required time and patience. It couldn't be forced to fit a certain pattern or time constraint. I could see that the Camino experience had extended into my day-to-day until now.

The liberation I felt was slow in unfolding over a number of weeks through the spring, as sunlight returned and nature switched back on. There was an undeniable sense of loss over a very worthwhile ministry that had been left behind, but there was a new joy in being set free, open to new possibilities, and setting my sights on new challenges. I had a strong sense of what I believe the disciples must have felt post-Resurrection, having felt that tremendous loss but somehow miraculously restored. The resurrection process is not something that has happened in the past once and for all, but it is happening now, continuously, the same process of death leading to new life. This is the process of our lives in faith, facing into the darkness and the seeming absence of God in order to experience him in a new way. Through the past year and a half, I had learned to respect this process, that the experience of dying can be crucial to how I experienced living.

The real Camino or pilgrimage is that of facing life's vagaries with good humor and patience, confident that God works within them, too. For me, the good life was no longer about perfection attained by my own efforts, ego-based control, or self-determined outreach and action. Rather, the good life exists in the much humbler path of having courage to make changes, realistically accepting limits, and maintaining faith in providence that God has a larger plan. Above all, though, it is in letting go of control and trusting in the slow unfolding of meaning.

I had fallen on the road in Spain and spent almost six months recovering from that injury and a year working through the subsequent discernment process. I was challenged, as my Jesuit training had taught me, to see God in the longer-term view and come to a new understanding. Initially, at least, it had proven difficult, as it was such a debilitating and apparently negative experience. It had often seemed as if God were absent or unavailable during this time of trial. None of the experience made sense without the Passion to read it by. I identified strongly with the naked humanity of Jesus on the cross, gasping the words, "My God, my God, why have you forsaken me?"[132] This revelation shows his fundamental solidarity with us in moments of trial and testing, such as those I had experienced. It also points the way and indicates how we should pray in those situations: a radical handing over of everything to the Father. What is apparently a lost and meaningless suffering becomes an important and definitive Christian revelation; by being faithful to God's will, we too will come to the light of the Resurrection.

God works most powerfully in the darkness and "death" on the cross.[133] I had found this out by my experience, bringing about

---

132. Matthew 27:46, citing Psalm 22.
133. Finding meaning in suffering means embracing the experience of the cross where we join our sufferings to those of the crucified Christ. Joseph A. Tetlow, SJ, "The

impossible new life and a new freedom, a transformed existence. Part of God's process for me, which was only made apparent at the end, was being taught patience in waiting for God's plan to unfold, the purification of false desires and motivations in letting go of bereavement ministry, and the instilling of a new prayer of "abandonment" and a closer sense of God's presence. Just like Ignatius of Loyola, I was a wounded pilgrim, physically but also psychologically and spiritually. This process was a constant reminder of my mortality and very human woundedness. I was lucky that my knee had healed after several months: it had afforded me the Ignatian insight of total reliance on God, committing myself to follow Christ.

I have to believe that Ignatius, the ultimate pilgrim, would have been quicker to recognize the clear signs of God in his own story. His goal of finding God in all things is nowhere more important than in human suffering. God is present, especially in difficulties, not in striving for self-created perfection. This is the reverse of the priorities and values that the world prizes (control, perfection, individualism, egoism). The apparent absence of God, though difficult for any of us to go through, is the litmus test of our faith, our motives, and our patience. Finding God in complex and often difficult situations is the challenge for today. Living with that connection, life is imbued with meaning and purpose. We can employ all our skills of intelligence, awareness, and reflection to separate the threads, through discernment, to live in the light.

These newly revealed interpretations, though paradoxical, have invested me with new life and purpose. I was helped to see how I was trying to control too much, how the "apparent goods" in bereavement ministry had become disordered attachments, and how I have a new awareness of the subtleties of discernment (how easy it was to

Language of the Cross," www.ignatianspirituality.com/the-language-of-the-cross/ (SE 191–198).

lose my way). I have been purified and have become a more aware pilgrim who trusts in a God of providence and the unexpected. God is in everything, no matter how unlikely. Suffering is inevitable for those who seek to live by love and the Gospel, not because you ask for it but because it is the cost of loving. It hollows us out, frees us of impurities, and allows us to be truer and more effective instruments of God's love. Life is an invitation to set out into the unknown and to walk this road with openness and humility.

Now, where did I put my backpack and boots . . .

EPILOGUE
FEELING GOOD

In 2018, a friend of mine brought me to see the new musical sensation from Belfast, Kaz Hawkins and her band. On my way home I was marveling at her rendition of a Nina Simone song, "Feelin' Good," which captured the exact spiritual emotion that I had at the end of my long two-year process. The themes of liberation, emancipation, and gradual wisdom stood out for me in this Gospel song. I understood that feeling good only came about with the integration of my experience on the trail with my experience back home. It had certainly been costly and hard-won wisdom, often coming out of confusion, negativity, and desolation. Ironically, pain had been a real teacher. Initially, my own drive and single-minded pursuit of the "Camino high" had taken over. Being a slave to how I expected to feel blinded me to the beauty of the moment and hindered my decision making.[134]

I had a sense of having been through a storm or purifying fire, the way of darkness. Injury and pain were the teachers that eventually brought me down to reality, and gradually to a deeper understanding. As the song says, the finding of peace or meaning, a sign of growth

---

134. This is close to the Ignatian concept of freedom as detachment or release from compulsions or addictions of all types, to be able to act in freedom and love as an instrument of the divine.

and healing, was only possible much later and with much reflection. I had found some new inner balance, no longer elated or spiritually "high" (as I had been after my 2011 Camino de Santiago pilgrimage) and neither dejected nor disillusioned. Rather, I was "soberly" happy, realistically engaged with life, having learnt a few hard lessons on the road. The people I had met on the way had also taught me some valuable lessons and put my own troubles into perspective. I understood how St. Ignatius benefitted from a similar process of enforced reflection; God finally managed to get through to him in convalescence, and he began to trust his experience.

I have tried to synthesize these paradoxical insights on my rocky road to recuperation into twelve points; they are loosely based on the 12 Steps of Alcoholics Anonymous, given their close connection to the *Spiritual Exercises*. The basic insight is that God is always working with us to help us overcome our addictive behaviors and destructive attachments and tendencies.[135]

1. **Live in the present.** It can be tempting to beat yourself up continually about the mistakes of the past, but the Spirit is more interested in the evolving present. Essentially, my failure to keep focus, getting distracted and living off memories, meant I couldn't be present to the moment. What makes this difficult are intrusive thoughts and ideas; keeping the mind quiet is the challenge. Gradually I learned to stop fighting with myself and accept the reality, messy as it was. There was no point in trying to make things otherwise. I was being taught how to recalibrate and trust my inner compass or GPS, i.e., judging my own pain and knowing when to quit the walk. I had to learn to stop trying to change reality and instead find God in the present, the

---

135. Jim Manney, "The Spiritual Exercises and the 12 Steps," www.ignatianspirituality.com/the-spiritual-exercises-and-the-12-steps/.

less than ideal moment where I found myself. Many other people I met along the way already had this insight. Paradoxically, peace came finally in embracing reality, seeing the gift in it, and learning how God worked through difficult experiences.

2. **Look beyond the dark night.** Even though I wouldn't have asked for it, there was some powerful learning through the fall, convalescence, and rehabilitation process. Initially it seemed so negative and destructive that I was tempted to blame God. It is always tempting to offload all responsibility onto a "controller" God. I knew it wasn't God that caused the fall, (I had to take a fair bit of responsibility for that), but once it had happened, it became a crucible of teaching. Especially in relation to inner freedom, I was continually invited to let go of things I was attached to (e.g., health, independence, suicide bereavement work). Ironically, I learned more in the dark and pain than I had ever done in the light. Getting injured became a gift when I looked back on it and saw the whole process. I had been complacent about being a pilgrim, thinking I knew it all, but here I was being taught by God in a new way, the way of darkness and (minor) disability.

3. **Forgive the mistakes of the past.** Looking back, I can see more clearly that I was a prisoner to expectations and feelings based on previous experiences on the Camino. Living in the past and dwelling on the losses reduced my openness to the wonder of future possibilities. Things didn't work out at all the way I wanted. I had ended up with an unexpected injury and a tedious recovery, and it took me a long time to face up to this and let go in freedom. I had canonized my previous Camino experiences and fell victim to continually comparing my present experience to those, which made the new one seem like a total disaster. Even though those had been originally good

experiences, in my disordered state they gradually became obstacles to my present peace. Forgiving myself and accepting God's love meant reconciling myself with the present challenges. I really wanted the same experience I'd had before, but every new day is an adventure into God's unknown and has to be allowed to develop. The essence of the Camino is openness to new routes, experiences, and people, not continually walking the same path, reliving an eternal Groundhog Day.

4. **Put community before the individual.** The way that people cropped up in my journey reminded me that I was not alone, others had much to teach me, and God worked through them. I had thought that physically walking the Camino on one's own was the hardest journey, but the most difficult is facing adversity and having to depend on others for assistance. The loss of independence is painful, but the gains to interacting with others are enormous. Being injured meant that I had to rely on others during the walk but especially in convalescence when I was almost totally dependent. Inevitably this meant placing trust in others, giving me an insight into those facing illness, dealing with disability, or battling inner demons. God is found in the concrete relationships, circumstances, and people of our world. Redemption and recovery are a humbling and sometimes messy communal process. The most unlikely people, planted in my path, were the source of greatest grace.

5. **Bring the Camino back home.** The distractions and busyness of ordinary life often serve to knock me off-balance, off the path, and into trouble. Walking my own road requires a focus and a concentration on God, often requiring purification of my motivations and my desire. Many forces act against my doing the good that I want, so I need to be able to fend off distractions, attacks, and seductive shortcuts or dead ends. This has a

lot more to do with my inner state of mind and awareness than anything external. Accordingly, physically walking the Camino de Santiago is easy as the path is given, compared with the daily pilgrimage of those who live with addictions, disabilities, darkness, and/or depression. Consciously taking those daily steps to walk in the light is another level of courage. The real Camino is tackling the landscape of my present life: the crossroads are key decision points, the backpack is the baggage of past hurts, biases, and patterns, and the human heart is the place of freedom, discernment, and dignity.

6. **Trust the process.** Recuperation for me was a slow, tedious process of literally taking small steps each day. My physiotherapist was very wise in telling me that being faithful to the exercises would eventually lead to healing. The same applies to spiritual life and wisdom; it is walked every day.[136] Even the highest-flown ideals and plans have to boil down to practical steps and incremental movements. Sometimes the start of a healing or renewal process is the hardest part of it. That is when it is full of real or imagined fears, which have to be confronted. That is when our trust that the path is leading somewhere is tested. A pilgrim is someone who continues to walk in spite of the darkness. He walks even when the path is unclear and sometimes when there is little immediate personal support or payoff. There are few witnesses to the everyday courage needed to get out of bed, to face your demons, and embrace the world. God works at this level too, knowing our thoughts and desires, and wanting to be part of our day in prayer.

---

136. Ignatius compares the Spiritual Exercises to physical exercises; a daily routine and structure eventually brings about great change (SE 1).

7. **Don't compare and despair.** The miracle for me was that my fall and the aftermath was very fruitful spiritually. I was tempted to compare myself to other hikers and see it as a disaster, but this was not helpful or true. Human progress is not measured in terms of accomplishments, awards, or kudos (e.g., Facebook likes) but in terms of a heart that is true, that can rise above adversity, and that is witness to compassion and love. I learned more in recuperation than I would have learned being successful. This mirrors St. Ignatius's experience to some extent. The idea of the journey is central to understanding that we can't get there at once, that development takes time and that everyone goes through tough moments. It means taking the longer view about joys, sorrows, and setbacks and understanding that we operate on God's time. What makes the difference is being rooted in your personal story, understanding that this is where God wants you to be, and discerning the next step.

8. **Remember that freedom is an inside job.** The hardest path is negotiating the labyrinth-like complexity of the human heart. The desires, motivations, and needs often operate below our consciousness until we are forced to confront them. Accidents such as falling on the Camino or coming down with the flu can be great moments of learning. They can uncover our attachments and presumptions, bringing us to greater awareness. My decision to withdraw from suicide bereavement work was unforeseen and challenging, but it ultimately worked out for the best. It was a moment of providential awareness like what St. Ignatius experienced during his convalescence in Loyola. Good decision making (discernment) was about making conflicting motivations explicit, deciding in freedom and awareness, and progressively learning from reflecting on that experience. Life teaches us all along the journey, as the Camino exemplifies,

if we can let go of control. Much "progress" happens in the darkness and hidden depths of the human soul, the inner, often painful process of purification. However, living and acting in freedom results in real joy, as I discovered in letting go of the burden and responsibility of suicide work.

9. **Experience the closeness of God.** My immobility after the fall and during recovery showed me clearly how close God was to me. Previously, I was often so active that I didn't realize this closeness. God waited until I was ready to listen to reveal his patient and gentle presence. I realized how everything I had taken for granted had actually been given to me, and it was God who took the lead. I realized afterwards that it was God who caught me. I discovered compassion and acceptance, not judgment. I realized it was a paradox: I was fundamentally fragile but gifted, and always held in God's love. Just as with the prodigal son's journey home, I was given multiple second chances and offered extraordinary forgiveness. Part of being injured was a process of purification: waiting in the silence and the darkness of the long nights, wondering if recovery would ever happen. Alternating between doubt and hope meant praying out of a deep need. Mostly it was about purifying my faith, though, shaking off complacency, shedding expectations, and coming to new understandings.

10. **Endure the silence of God.** Silence is most harrowing when passing through difficult times. It is like facing the apparent absence of God or being abandoned by him. For me, this was the long hours of immobility and persistent low feelings. Of course, it does not necessarily mean the absence of God, but it sure feels like that. Left to my own devices, with too much idle time, my mind gets overactive. Ignatius outlines several reasons for this desolation: it can mean we had forgotten God and

maybe unconsciously relied on our own resources too much or got complacent about consolation, or it can be an invitation to purify unhelpful aspects of our faith and forge a new mature one. I took great heart in imagining Jesus in his Passion; he obviously felt emotionally the abandonment of God, but his faith told him that there was something else happening. And this proved to be the pivotal moment where God worked most powerfully in resurrecting him, overcoming death, and giving meaning to suffering as an act of love. Nowhere is God more present to Jesus and more powerfully working than that moment on the cross; similarly for us, those paradoxically dark moments can be transformative.

11. **Receive God's amazing grace.** I probably didn't do enough physical preparation or clarify the reasons for why I was going back to the Camino, and I took a number of shortcuts along the way. However, despite everything that went wrong, the good finally did win out. This was true especially in terms of my knee healing but also in terms of spiritual insights. Retiring from suicide bereavement work was, in retrospect, the most important decision based on my new understanding of how to make better decisions. Through everything, God didn't give up on me; there was grace even in my apparent failure. Looking back over it all now, I realize God was working through all of this entire healing journey, even when I was distracted and disillusioned. I was continually invited to change some lesser motivations (i.e., reliving the glory days, getting kudos) in an ongoing purification process. The people I met especially reminded me of how blessed I actually was and how I needed to focus on staying open for God's unfolding plan. At the time it was hard to believe God was working through difficult situations. Getting injured presented the hidden luxury of extended reflection, as

Ignatius himself found out. There were some things under my control, like the unhelpful expectations and desires, but everything else had to be handed over to God to make something out of it.

12. **We are part of God's creation.** I need to continually remember that I am a child of God and keep on track despite the unpredictable vagaries and alluring detours of life. It is so easy to get isolated, lose hope, and buy into the secular hype. Living out the Camino attitudes of trust, openness, and flexibility is a major challenge at home with all its constraints and tedium, and yet all the opportunities, interactions, and decision moments are still there. I had to continually make the effort to get back on the path of positivity and consolation, recognizing the dangers posed by negativity, the ego, and false motivations. Following in the footsteps of Ignatius meant practicing daily meditation, reflection, openness to the other, inner freedom, and trust in providence. The modern Western world often conspires against this possibility, insisting that you are an isolated individual, that there is no meaning in life (and thus, no Camino), and that continuous consumerism is all we can hope for. But the divine spark inside never extinguishes.

To quote Kaz Hawkins, in conclusion, "Freedom is mine, and I know how I feel." It's a funny world and even funnier the way things worked out. On one level, I may be the unluckiest pilgrim in the world, but then again, as Anthony de Mello says, "Good luck, bad luck, who knows?" I often jokingly say that to be a real Jesuit you have to limp across Spain on a bad leg like St. Ignatius! There are some learnings that are made possible by situations of failure, where the pressing reality forces us to integrate our faith through our very body. This embodied spirituality, living faith concretely as Jesus did, is what the

Camino experience forces us through. Nonetheless, God is with us all at every moment, in all things, and even in difficult situations.

Personally, I have no doubt that I was being freed of my crippling expectations and desires and that the physical recuperation also included a spiritual process of rebuilding and purification. Experiencing disability and recuperation were key parts of this, unpleasant at times and unasked for, but God worked powerfully through that. Subsequently, letting go of the suicide bereavement work was the litmus test of my inner freedom, the end of the process. Now, I am certainly more aware of my own limitations and failings and my dependence on God's love and grace for living well in the world. I have learned not to waste time worrying about why things are happening to me but rather to be present to what is happening now and what decisions I have to make going forward. "Feeling good" is great when it happens but not central to walking the journey of faith.

IGNATIAN TIPS
 *for*
FEELING GOOD

1. There is a GPS buried deep in us that always points to the good, but we have to work to get in sync with it. God is in our deepest desires, not the superficial ones; we have to sift desires and motivations to make sure we follow the most life-giving ones. God helps us with this work of separating or discerning through the gift of our emotions and affectivity.

2. Be grateful for what you have received, for the past blessings, but be open to the possibilities of a new day. Take time each day to reflect on your experience (i.e., the Examen). Be grateful for the past but not caught in it. Ignatius used to say that ingratitude is the greatest sin; it will also destroy your peace of mind.

3. We live in a manic world and easily get hooked into roller-coaster emotional rides, thrilling but costly. Stay away from extremes; look, rather, for the point of balance, where there is genuine peace to be had.

4. Use physical things, money, technology, etc., insofar as they bring us to God, to inner peace, and to the service of others; avoid becoming subservient to technology, social media, money, and wealth. These things can easily become forms of egoism or addiction, states in which we are unfree.

5. Good decision making is key: Take time over important decisions, pray with them, talk them over with a trusted friend, and gather all the necessary information. Depersonalize a decision by asking yourself how you would advise someone else making that same decision.

6. Be careful seeing decisions through; they may take time and commitment, and we can lose heart implementing them. Remember Ignatius's rules of thumb for decision making: trust your feelings but use your head, don't change course midstream, don't go back on good decisions.

7. In really difficult and painful times, unavoidable suffering, gracefully borne, will lead to God. We have to dig deep and find a way through, being faithful to our decisions and commitments, even though often it doesn't feel great. Think of Jesus' faithfulness to love on the cross. The challenge in this case is to put one's superficial feelings to one side (i.e., seeking comfort or escape) and hang on, but also remembering that when God appears absent, these moments can lead to the greatest freedom, liberation, and insight.

8. Glorifying suffering and not taking measures to alleviate it is often not helpful or from God either. We have to do everything in our power to get information, get help on problems, and take the necessary steps to alleviate or correct them. All the rest belongs to God.

APPENDIX
PRAYING WITH FAILURE

Bring to mind the often unpleasant experience of failure, sit with it, try to find an image that captures it for you.

Admit your vulnerability or sometimes helplessness in the face of this experience.

Acknowledge that you need God's help: make it real, not just asking a remote god but pleading with a living, breathing, concerned, and compassionate God.

Make your own petition for what you need in your own words, for example: "God, I really screwed it up this time. I really can't cope, and I desperately need some help." Feel the weight of your need or desire in your words.

Picture Jesus on the cross and try to connect emotionally with his awful Passion, his whole project having failed, his friends having turned against him, having been betrayed by a friend, and abandoned by all but a few. But . . . he found a way through, abandoning himself to God (using the words of the Psalms: "into your hand I commit"), by being faithful in prayer and believing against all odds that the power of God transformed this situation. All the violence, evil, and hatred was transformed into forgiveness and compassion; death or disaster was not the end. In fact, it was a new beginning.

Use your imagination to hand your failure over to Jesus to have it transformed; it takes complete trust and commitment.

Try to picture your failure transformed: what would it mean for you to have it "pass through fire," what would the gift in the experience be, how would you live differently? What does God want for you out of this experience, how would it look through the eyes of God who has walked through the fire with you?

PLAYLIST OF SONGS

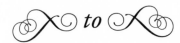 *to*

ACCOMPANY THIS BOOK

1. "Blinded by the Light," Manfred Mann's Earth Band, *The Roaring Silence*, 1976.
2. "Walking on Sunshine," Katrina and the Waves, *Walking on Sunshine*, 1983.
3. "Bonny Portmore," Loreena McKennitt, *The Visit*, 1991.
4. "Sanctuary," Secret Garden, *White Stones*, 1997.
5. "Misty Mountain Hop," Led Zeppelin, *Led Zeppelin IV*, 1971.
6. "Kalera noa ihesi," Oskorri, *Hamabost Urte Eta Gero Hau*, 2006.
7. "Wayfaring Stranger," Jack White, *Cold Mountain* (Soundtrack to *Cold Mountain* movie), 2003.
8. "Noraezean," *Hesian*, Hitzetik, 2011.
9. "By the Rivers of Babylon," Boney M, *Nightflight to Venus*, 1978.
10. "Red Red Wine," UB40, *Labour of Love*, 1983.
11. "Take My Breath Away," Berlin, *Top Gun* (Soundtrack to *Top Gun* movie), 1986.
12. "György Ligeti," *Volumina*, Organ Solo, 1966.
13. "Song for Someone," U2, *Songs of Innocence*, 2014.

14. "La Sagrada Familia," Alan Parsons Project, *Gaudi*, 1987.

15. "Love Is a Losing Game," Amy Winehouse, *Back to Black*, 2006.

16. "The Silence of God," Andrew Peterson, *After All These Years*, 2014.

17. "Give Me Novacaine," Green Day, *American Idiot*, 2004.

18. "Belfast Blues," The Felsons, *Glad*, 1998.

19. "One," U2, *Achtung Baby*, 1991.

20. "Everybody Hurts," REM, *Automatic for the People*, 1992.

21. "Feelin' Good," Kaz Hawkins Band, *Feelin' Good*, 2016.

This playlist, entitled "The Road to Manresa," is available through Spotify or through the author's Facebook page.

SELECT REFERENCES
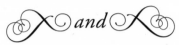 *and*
RECOMMENDED READING

Barry, William A., SJ. "Finding God in All Things," extracted from
www.ignatianspirituality.com/13598/
god-is-trying-to-catch-our-attention

Barry, William A., SJ, and Connolly, William J., SJ. *The Practice of Spiritual Direction*. San Francisco: Harper San Francisco, 1982.

Brodrick, James. *Saint Ignatius Loyola: The Pilgrim Years, 1491–1538*. San Francisco: Ignatius Press, 1998.

Carver, Joseph, SJ. *Ignatian Spirituality and Ecology: Entering into Conversation with the Earth*. Jesuit Higher Education: A Journal. Vol. 4, No. 2, Article 10. https://epublications.regis.edu/

English, John J. *Spiritual Freedom: From an Experience of the Ignatian Exercises to the Art of Spiritual Guidance*. 2nd ed. Chicago: Loyola Press, 1995.

Fleming, David L. *Draw Me into Your Friendship—The Spiritual Exercises: A Literal Translation and a Contemporary Reading*. St. Louis: Institute of Jesuit Sources, 1996.

Frankl, Viktor E. *Man's Search for Meaning: An Introduction to Logotherapy*. New York: Simon & Schuster, 1984.

Green, Thomas H. *Weeds among the Wheat*. Notre Dame, IN: Ave Maria Press, 1984.

Grogan, Brian. *Alone and on Foot: Ignatius of Loyola*. Dublin: Veritas, 2009.

Harter, Michael, ed. *Hearts on Fire: Praying with Jesuits*. Chicago: Loyola Press, 2005.

Hughes, Gerard W. *In Search of a Way: Two Journeys of Spiritual Discovery*. London: Darton, Longman and Todd, 1986.

Ignatian Camino Website: www.caminoignaciano.org/en/.

Ignatian Spirituality Website: www.ignatianspirituality.com.

Iriberri, José Luis, SJ, and Lowney, Chris. *Guide to the Camino Ignaciano*. Bilbao, Spain: Mensajero, 2017.

Ivens, Michael. *An Approach to Saint Ignatius of Loyola*. Edited by Joseph Munitiz. Oxford: Way Books, 2008.

Ivens, Michael. *Understanding the Spiritual Exercises*. Leominster, England: Gracewing, 1998.

Ivereigh, Austen. *The Great Reformer: Francis and the Making of a Radical Pope*. London: Allen & Unwin, 2014.

Lonsdale, David. *Dance to the Music of the Spirit: The Art of Discernment*. London: Darton, Longman and Todd, 1992.

Lowney, Chris. *Heroic Leadership*. Chicago: Loyola Press, 2003.

Martin, James, SJ. *The Jesuit Guide to (Almost) Everything*. New York: HarperOne, 2010.

McManus, Brendan, SJ. "Ignatian Pilgrimage: The Inner Journey—Loyola to Manresa on Foot." *The Way* 9, no. 3 (July 2010).

Meissner, W. W. *Ignatius of Loyola: The Psychology of a Saint*. New Haven: Yale University, 1992.

Modras, Ronald. *Ignatian Humanism: A Dynamic Spirituality for the 21st Century*. Chicago: Loyola Press, 2004.

Muldoon, Tim. *The Ignatian Workout: Daily Spiritual Exercises for a Healthy Faith*. Chicago: Loyola Press, 2004.

Munitiz, Joseph. "St. Ignatius of Loyola and Severe Depression." *The Way* 44, no. 3 (July 2005): 58–59.

Navone, John J. *Triumph through Failure: A Theology of the Cross*. Eugene, OR: WIPF & Stock, 1984.

O'Brien, Kevin, SJ. *The Ignatian Adventure*. Chicago: Loyola Press, 2011.

O'Leary, Brian. *Ignatian Spirituality*. Dublin: Messenger Publications, 2009.

O'Mahony, Gerald. *Finding the Still Point*. Guilford, England: Eagle Publishing, 1992.

O'Sullivan, Michael. "Trust Your Feelings, but Use Your Head." *Studies in the Spirituality of Jesuits*, 22, no. 4 (1990).

Pope Francis. *The Joy of the Gospel: Evangelii Gaudium*. Frederick, MD: Word among Us Press, 2014.

Reites, James. "Ignatius and Ministry with Women," in *Women and Ignatian Spirituality in Dialogue*, *The Way*, Supplement No. 74, (1992), pp. 7–19.

Rotsaert, Mark, SJ. "Obedience in the Life of the Society of Jesus," GC 35 Decree 4, *Review of Ignatian Spirituality*, XL, 1/2009, pp. 26–36.

Savary, Louis M. *The New Spiritual Exercises: In the Spirit of Pierre Teihlard de Chardin*. Mahwah, NJ: Paulist Press, 2010.

Sheppard, Jim, SJ. "'See, Judge, Act' And Ignatian Spirituality," *The Way*, 56/1 (January 2017), pp. 102–111.

Silf, Margaret. *Inner Compass: An Invitation to Ignatian Spirituality*. Chicago: Loyola Press, 1998.

Tylenda, Joseph N. *A Pilgrim's Journey: The Autobiography of Ignatius of Loyola*. Collegeville, MN: Liturgical Press, 1991.

Yancey, Philip. *Disappointment with God*. Grand Rapids, MI: Zondervan, 1988.

ACKNOWLEDGMENTS

Thanks to my Jesuit provincial, Leonard Moloney, SJ, for having faith in me; for Brian Grogan, SJ, and the Leeson Street community for a wonderful airy loft and solitude to write; for the Jesuit community in Belfast for always supporting me (even in tetchy moments). For my family who have always been there for me. Thanks also to Fr. Michael Spence and St. Malachy's Seminary, Belfast, for providing me with a place to edit.

Specifically, I want to thank Karen Rossignol and Conall O'Cuinn for their committed editing and constructive critique; Pat McGuinness for her proofreading; and also Pat Coyle for her help in focusing and clarifying the direction of the book. Also, Loyola Press and the staff who have been great supporters, especially my excellent general editor, Gaston Philipps, director, Maria Cuadrado, and copy editor, Katherine Faydash. Thanks to Terry Howard, SJ, for advice on the route, Tony O'Riordan, SJ, for email support, and Jim Deeds for support on the journey, especially for the ideas behind *Finding God in the Mess*. I owe a debt of gratitude to Jo Murphy and Conor McCafferty of Lighthouse and Claire Dowds of Bethany for their unwavering support for and assistance with working in suicide bereavement ministry. Thanks to Niall Leahy, SJ, and the Irish MAGIS group for carrying me along on their enthusiasm, and also our Polish leaders

Wojciech Kowalski, SJ, Magda Gosiąrowska, Bartłomiej Lisek, Kasia Wilk, and Paweł Wilk.

Mostly, I am greatly indebted to those that I met on the road who taught me and helped me and are the real stars of this book. I know it's not fair to single out Enric, SJ, my Barcelona contact; Cecilia, the physiotherapist who first spotted the issue; the A&E doctor who made the crucial diagnosis; Patrick, my faithful driver; Maeve, for the A&E pickup; Glen, the rehabilitation physiotherapist; Tim, for the Manchester invitation; Billy, who introduced me to Kaz Hawkins; Gerry, for his constant friendship; Colin, for friendship and a place to write; the wonderful NHS system, who looked after me so well; the Eek family, for hospitality; Davy, for the coffees; and my Facebook friends, who gave me lots of useful advice. Special appreciation is due to my brother Donal, who was with me in a new way on this journey.

Thanks to José Luis Irriberri, SJ, for all his assistance, particularly for permission to use the Ignatian Camino route map; also to Jakub Nicieja, for permission to reproduce the concert photo from MAGIS 2016.

Disclaimer: I have tried to recreate events, locales, and conversations from my memories of them. In order to maintain their anonymity, in some instances I have changed the names of individuals and places. I may have also changed some identifying characteristics and details such as physical properties, occupations, and places of residence.